DATE			

Traditional
and Folk Puppets
of the World

Also by MICHAEL R. MALKIN:

The Unpredictable Mr. Punch
The Barber of Seville (Translation/Adaptation)

Traditional
and Folk Puppets
of the World

Michael R. Malkin

With Photographs by David L. Young

Additional Photographs by Alan G. Cook

South Brunswick and New York: A. S. Barnes and Company
London: Thomas Yoseloff Ltd

A. S. Barnes and Co., Inc.
Cranbury, New Jersey 08512

Thomas Yoseloff Ltd
Magdalen House
136-148 Tooley Street
London SE1 2TT, England

Library of Congress Cataloging in Publication Data

Malkin, Michael R.   1943-
  Traditional and folk puppets of the world.

  Bibliography: p.
  Includes index.
  1. Puppets and puppet-plays. I. Title.
PN1972.M32   745.59'22   76-26381
ISBN 0-498-01871-7

For Pam, with love

Printed in the United States of America

Contents

Acknowledgments

I am indebted to a large number of people for their advice, support, and assistance in the preparation of this book: to Daniel Llords for information and photos; to the Reverend Jack Lipman, S.J. of Sinchu, Taiwan, for information on Chinese hand puppetry; to Ellen Proctor and Audley Grossman of the Detroit Institute of the Arts for providing access to the Puppet Collection; to Mrs. Meher R. Contractor of New Delhi for supplying rare and valuable material on Indian puppetry; to Dr. Mel Helstien of the University of California, Los Angeles, for advice and for providing access to items in his collection; to Raul Lopez of the Museum of Cultural History at UCLA for providing access to certain photographs; to Margo Lovelace of Pittsburgh, Pennsylvania, for information and assistance in photographing items in her collection; to John U. Zweers of Pasadena, California, for photographs of figures in his collection; to Thomas K. Seligman of the M. H. deYoung Museum in San Francisco for help in obtaining a photograph of a *temes nevinbur* figure; to John Mebane, editor of *The Antiques Journal,* who kindly allowed reprinting of material that originally appeared in that magazine; to J. and L. Contryn of Belgium for their information on the puppets of Belgium and Northern France; to Ria Rowe of the Museum of Anthropology at the University of British Columbia for assistance in obtaining photographs of items in the Museum collection; to Robert A. Elder, Jr. of the National Museum of Natural History for aid in locating and photographing *hula ki'i* figures; and to the staff of the Smithsonian Institution for their assistance. Particular gratitude is due to Don Avery, editor of *The Puppetry Journal,* for his flow of invaluable advice, inspiration and support; to Thomas Goodrich of Indiana, Pennsylvania, for permission to use photographs of his Turkish shadow figures; to Alan G. Cook of North Hollywood, California, for his many photographs of the puppets in his spectacular collection as well as his knowledge, time, and labor; and to David L. Young of Indiana, Pennsylvania, whose superb photographs fill these pages.

Without question, it is to my wife and colleague, Pamela Malkin, to whom I am most deeply grateful, for her patience, editorial advice, intelligent criticism, and energetic involvement concerning every aspect of the preparation of this book.

Introduction

For many of us, puppets belong to a world of alphabet blocks, little red wagons, and rainy Saturday recollections of squeaky voices and tangled strings. It seems self-evident that just about everyone has played with puppets and that virtually no one takes them seriously. As a result, very few people notice when theater historians, theater critics, and even puppeteers themselves unwittingly perpetuate a subtle and unfortunate myth: namely, that puppet theater is essentially a children's art form that is, occasionally, unnaturally, extended in order to cater to more mature artistic awarenesses.

Not surprisingly, many of the increasing number of fine books and articles on the history and aesthetics of puppetry leave a reader with the impression that the art is little more than a minor theatrical oddity. The September 1972 "Puppet" issue of *The Drama Review* was a case in point. The editors of that issue went so far as to put the word *puppet* in quotation marks because the term, in their view, did not "describe satisfactorily . . . the concepts of the inanimate actor, depersonalization, incarnation, and so forth."[1] It is as though the editors were convinced that the word *puppet,* without quotation marks, represented too elementary a concept or too naive an art form for their purposes. The articles treated the puppet as mask, the puppet as symbol, the actor as puppet, and so forth, but there was no attempt to articulate any contemporary concept of the puppet as puppet.

The fault is not the exclusive property of the editors of *The Drama Review.* The idea that puppetry may be one of the roots as opposed to one of the branches of theater is rarely given serious consideration.

In order to develop this idea, it will be necessary to isolate certain basic characteristics of the actor, the mask, and the puppet.

The actor is the primary source of theatrical energy. He has his intelligence, his voice, his gestures, his movement, and his language. For our purposes, the actor is also singer and dancer. He usually uses makeup and costume to help the audience respond to him. A particular virtue of the actor as actor is the nature of his relationship with his audience. Even when he is playing a bear or a flower he remains quintessentially human and the audience appreciates his performance while accepting that perception. The audience looks on the actor directly but shares his projected vision of himself.

At some point, it is impossible to say precisely how or when, the actor attains a certain level of aesthetic abstraction. Something is interposed between him and his audience. This something partakes of mystery, ritual, symbol, and the intellect. The actor no longer projects himself directly to the audience but through some *thing* or *concept* called a mask. It is important to distinguish the *thing* mask from the *concept* mask because, although they are intimately related, they can exist quite independently of one another. The *thing* mask is an object that disguises and conceals. The *concept* mask is an idea that can suggest or express something about the actor and his performance that was not there before. Specifically, the *concept* mask implies the existence of a particular kind of indirect or abstract relationship between the actor and the audience. Jerzy Growtowski's actors of The Polish Laboratory Theatre have achieved this kind of effect without *thing* masks by exercising tremendous control over the muscles of their faces and bodies.

There is a fascinating aesthetic proximity between the actor and his mask. The audience can see the mask only as the actor presents it, and they can see the actor only through the mask. The mask is hard, sculptured, and immutable but the audience is always aware of the life behind it—the creative forces that maintain it and are the reasons for its existence. The actor's stage role is welded to the mask. His relationship with it is intense and intimate but never face to face. Although he may hold it in his hands and examine it, he must step into it from behind.

Beyond the mask is the puppet. The puppet is both perceived and presented at a more abstract level than the mask. It is both literally and figuratively further from the actor than the mask. This additional distance is crucial because it depersonalizes the actor; that is, the audience no longer perceives him. They can relate to the puppet as object, symbol, or concept in a very direct way but they have little or no desire to find the human being who is behind or beneath or above it. In fact, quite the reverse happens. The audience unconsciously severs its perceptions of the actor and responds to the puppet as pure theatrical abstraction. The audience's reference point shifts from the actor to the things he manipulates. As a result, even if he is not invisible to the eyes of the audience members, the actor is almost entirely excluded—as human being—from their consciousness.

For his part, the actor in performance is seldom closer to his puppet than arm's length and he is often a good deal further away than that. Purely mechanical things—wires, strings, rods, controls—are interposed between the actor and his role. When properly and imaginatively conceived, these mechanical contrivances must be viewed as refinements and not as obstacles or encumbrances in the way of artistic expression. They allow the actor to control his creation while simultaneously withdrawing from it. As he withdraws, he can become both more flexible and more objective. In this way, the creation and operation of puppets can become both an exquisite and rarified expression of the actor's art and a primary mode of theater.

Like most art forms, puppet theater is sometimes remarkably crude and sometimes quite refined. From time to time, it has been successful as both cabaret-style entertainment and sophisticated theater. In recent years, television and puppetry have shown an extraordinary compatibility.

Nonetheless, for thousands of years, puppetry has been particularly popular as either a traditional and highly developed form of entertainment for a wealthy or aristocratic elite, or as folk theater—a theater of and for the people—with its stock characters, standard bits of stage business, lively plots, and raucous, good humor. As is the case with much traditional and folk art, the artists themselves have often been virtually anonymous—obscured by the vigorous theatrical traditions of which they are only a small part.

Along with the puppeteers, the theaters, and the techniques of performance, the puppets themselves are significant elements of these traditions. Whether delicately fashioned to suit the tastes of the rich and powerful or boldly created for the rigors of popular performance, they are often superb examples of the craftsman's skill. There are, for instance, the exquisitely frail shadow figures of China, the regal and subtle puppets of Japan's Bunraku theater, the elemental crudeness of Turkey's Karagoz, and, of course, the color and comic grotesqueness of Punch and Judy.

These and the other puppet theater characters and traditions that will be discussed in this book have three features in common. First, they are rooted in the beliefs, legends, and customs of their parent cultures. Second, they have endured for more than one generation. Third, the performances represent the creation and expression of cultural traditions rather than the unique achievements of an individual puppeteer or troupe of puppeteers.

This book is intended as a summary of traditional and folk puppetry around the world. While it is as complete and accurate as I could make it, it is by no means an exhaustive scholarly study. Decisions as to what information to include and what not to include were based on my personal judgment of what would be of the most interest to those with a general interest in puppetry and folk theater. In fact, if it answers a few questions, offers some clues for future scholarly inquiry, and, most of all, provides a modicum of inspiration for present and future puppeteers, this book will have more than fulfilled its purpose.

NOTES

1. Michael Kirby, "Introduction," "The 'Puppet' Issue," *The Drama Review*, ed. Michael Kirby. 16(1972): 3.

Traditional
and Folk Puppets
of the World

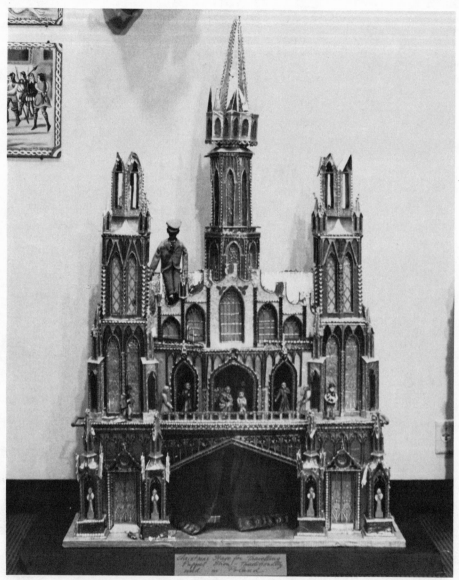

Polish puppet stage or *szupka* **made in the 1960s to resemble a church. Note stage opening at bottom center and a puppet from a larger** *szupka* **sitting near left tower.** *Courtesy Alan G. Cook. (Photo by Alan G. Cook)*

1

European Traditional Puppets

A harried family pauses for a few moments to laugh at the tiny figures performing in an out of the way corner of the market plaza. The jaded sophisticate accompanied by a sumptuously appareled lady friend drifts toward the small and gaily colored booth set up in front of a flowering rhododendron in a sunny city park. A gnarled and heavily muscled laborer joins his companions in a small, meagerly lighted theater beneath the neighborhood bakery in an anonymous urban back street. Wandering down the narrow lanes lined with hundreds of gravelly voiced hucksters loudly extolling the merits of their bargain wares, two children tug at their father's sleeve. They beg to stop for a while to watch and listen to a strange, reedy-voiced little fellow with a huge hooked nose.

They are, all of them, irresistibly attracted to puppet shows. At some times defying the legal restrictions of city and state, at other times ignoring the warnings of the clergy and always blissfully immune to literary pretention and prejudice, Europe's folk puppeteers apparently have usually known how and where to find their audiences.

There are many fine studies of the European puppet theater. George Speaight's *History of the English Puppet Theatre*, published in 1955, is among the best. Despite its title, it is an excellent history of European—as well as English—puppetry. Together with his *History of the English Toy Theatre* and *Punch and Judy: A History*, which is a reworking of *History of the English Puppet Theatre*, Speaight's works stand as outstanding contributions to the history of puppet theater in Europe. In addition, more than half of René Simmen's beautifully illustrated book, *The World of Puppets*, published in German in 1972 and in English in 1975, is devoted to a discussion of European puppetry.

Speaight notes that:

> The history of puppets is a long one. They had certainly appeared on the European scene by five hundred years before the birth of Christ, when there is evidence of their use for entertainment in Greece; they were already established in Sicily by that date, and they were popular and frequently commented upon by Latin authors during the period of the Roman republic and empire. Two main types of puppet appear to have been known: marionettes and glove puppets. The marionette is a full-length jointed figure, moved from above by a stout wire to the head and strings to the hands (the all-stringed marionette did not evolve until the nineteenth century); according to Apuleius, writing in A.D. 200, Roman marionettes could even roll their eyes. . . .
> Both of these kinds of figures continued in use throughout the Middle Ages, performed by minstrels and jongleurs and occasionally in crib plays and other religious dramas.[1]

Apparently, despite the intermittent opposition of the clergy, both religious and secular puppetry were quite popular as early as the twelfth century. Toys and portable puppet booths were to be seen in market plazas and occasionally in church squares and primitive *marionnettes à la planchette* were also quite popular. *Marionnettes à la planchette* were articulated figures that were operated by means of a single, horizontal string that was tied around the performer's knee, passed through the chest of the puppet and then tied to a post. Most often, this post was attached to a plank that also acted as a floor for the dancing or "jigging" puppet. Since the performer's hands were left free, he would usually also play an instrument such as a guitar or the bagpipes. By moving his leg in time to the music, the puppeteer would make the puppet dance while the noise of the figure's feet on the plank flooring provided a rhythmic visual and tympanic accompaniment to the music.

Between the twelfth and fourteenth centuries, traveling entertainers in northern Germany enlivened their performances by the use of simple hand puppets called *kobolds* or *tattermen*.[2] It is unclear whether or not these figures were articulated. The mock scepters of the medieval fool—called *marottes*—may also have been used as simple rod puppets. A *marotte* usually consisted of a short rod with a wooden fool's head attached to the upper end.[3]

Some scholars believe that puppets were important in the performance of medieval mystery and morality plays. Both Bil Baird[4] and Marjorie Batchelder[5] refer to an elaborate ceremony called "The Mysteries of Mid-August" that is said to have occurred in 1443 at the Church of St. James at Dieppe. The performance included God the

Nineteenth-century Belgian rod puppets. Their costumes indicate that they represent reasonably prosperous country characters. The figures have been reconstructed several times. *Courtesy John U. Zweers. (Photo by John U. Zweers)*

Father, a number of large and small angels who flapped their wings while suspended in midair, a figure of the Virgin, and a clown called Grimpe-Sur-l'Ais. Some of these figures ascended and descended through the air and were capable of a wide range of movement. Although this performance has occasionally been described as a high point in medieval puppet theater, it is, in fact, not precisely clear which of the characters were mechanical figures or automata, which were puppets, and which were live actors. Nonetheless, it seems more than likely that puppets had at least some place in the religious dramas of the Middle Ages.

For example, it is known that puppets were widely used in various kinds of dramatic representations of the nativity. The most famous of the puppet nativity plays are the Polish *szupka*, which have been performed in an unbroken tradition since the thirteenth century. *Szupka* puppets are controlled with a single stick or wire and are used on elaborate stages with two acting levels that are made to resemble churches. The operators stand behind the stage and manipulate the

Belgian string and rod puppet lady probably dating from the late nineteenth century. *Courtesy Alan G. Cook. (Photo by Alan G. Cook)*

figures along slots or grooves in the stage floor. Most of the characters are modeled after traditional roles in the medieval mystery and morality plays: devils, angels, and Death, as well as upon regional and ethnic types:

There is a Pole with a long moustache and a sword, a swarthy Ukranian, a short haired German, a gay Krakowian in high boots and a red cap pushed over one ear, a Caparthian mountaineer and a Gypsy. Each is accompanied by his wife, and they dance to the accompaniment of favorite songs.[6]

Originally given in monasteries, performances eventually became more popular and by the seventeenth century, *szupka* performances were in vogue at fairs and market places as well as in churches.[7]

In the Russian Ukraine, there is a similar form of puppet nativity play called the *vertiep* or *bertep*—meaning Bethlehem. It, too, is still played on elaborate two-level stages that resemble domed, Eastern churches. The upper level is used for nativity scenes and the lower level for more secular farces and fantasies. Each level has one central exit and the entire theater, according to tradition, should be illuminated with candlelight during performances.

Another form related to the *szupka* and called the *crèche parlante* or talking crib, became popular in Provençe toward the end of the eighteenth century. The figures were made of wax and were movable. According to one source, the *crèche parlant* stage was:

> . . . composed of a series of inclined planes, ordinarily numbered five, upon which are moved marionettes of different heights according to the plane upon which they are found, in such a way as to produce a perfect illusion for the spectator. The largest measure 70 cm. and the smallest only 20, although they appear of greater stature. In the old cribs, these characters are remarkable for their mechanism and modelling. The figures and the hands, usually of wax, are fine and without flaw.
>
> Instead of being moved by strings attached to the head, arms and legs like string marionettes, these dolls are put into motion by a mechanism hidden in the body of the figure, which is mounted on a wooden rod. To make the puppets move on the desired level, the wooden block to which they are fastened slides on the proper plane, so that their feet just clear the scenery. In certain cribs, the pedestal was even mounted on little wheels which glided on rails.
>
> Heads and arms, sometimes eyes and mouths, can be raised, lowered, opened or closed at will, thanks to small springs controlled by fine cords of gut, fixed to metal rings which pass to the fingers of the operator. As Charles Martin observes, the system which fixes the little cords to the keys is preferable because in pressing upon them, the gut is stretched and the spring thus controlled makes the head, the arms or the legs move at will, according to the poem or song.[8]

As with the *szupka, crèche parlant* plays were usually concerned with the events surrounding the birth of Christ. Both the *crèches parlant* and the *szupkas* are, in large measure, outgrowths of the taste for mechanical figures and entertainments that began to develop in Europe during the Middle Ages.

This interest in mechanics accounts for the popularity, particularly in the eighteenth and ninteenth centuries, of a number of theaters that

Late nineteenth- or early twentieth-century Belgian string and rod puppet of a priest. *Courtesy Margo Lovelace. (Photo by David L. Young)*

were called variously peep shows, puppet shows, and mechanical spectacles. Occasionally, such performances were combinations of these various traditions and techniques.

The simplest of these forms was the portable peep show. This was a box containing cut-out pictures of well-known locations complete with people, buildings, trees, and animals. Customers could view the scene through a small peephole in the box. Usually, the peep shows required daylight but many of them were equipped with special lanterns for nighttime viewing. Also called raree shows, these entertainments were forerunners in style, if not in fact, to the paper and cardboard toy theaters that became popular in nineteenth-century England and Austria. Sometimes, raree shows were animated in part by simple machinery and in part by the hands of the operator, who could move certain elements of the scenes by means of rods that were concealed in special slots in the bottom or sides of the theaters.

More elaborate mechanical theaters were used by traveling puppeteers in conjunction with their own shows. Known as *theatrum mundi*, such displays were used as early as the sixteenth century. Max von Boehn has noted that:

> The *theatrum mundi* for centuries provided the traditional afterpieces of the wandering marionette theatres; by means of small moveable figures running on rails, it showed a diversity of scenes, such as the creation of the world and Noah and the Flood. Flocton's show, which was exhibited in England at the end of the eighteenth century, utilized five hundred figures, all employed in different ways and manners. Here there were moveable figures of a peculiarly ingenious kind: swans, for example, which dipped their heads in the water, spread their wings, and craned their long necks to clean their feathers.[9]

Superb photographs of such figures can be found in Günter Böhmer's *The Wonderful World of Puppets*.[10] Some of the *theatrum mundi* figures were cast in metal, some were carved in wood, and others were simply cut in profile out of cardboard. In every case, the great attraction of the form was the degree of skill and mechanical ingenuity with which the figures were made to move.

Yet another type of traveling street puppet show became particularly popular in England after 1830. These galanty shows, as they were known, were portable theaters in which a sheer white fabric was stretched across the opening of a hand puppet booth and then lighted from behind. Cut out wood or cardboard figures were then manipulated against the illuminated screens. This form of puppet show is sometimes confused in literary references with magic lantern entertainments, in which translucent paintings on glass slides were set into a special lantern and projected against a screen.[11]

Because generations of itinerant showmen were far less precise in their use of words than subsequent generations of scholars have wished, it is often quite difficult to decide what kind of show was performed at a particular time or place. For example, the term *marionette* was often applied to any kind of puppet—whether hand, string, or rod—and the word *motion* seems at one time or another to have been used to describe every conceivable type of puppet, automaton, peep show, or *theatrum mundi*.

Other European puppets that have their roots in medieval or even Greek and Roman theatricals are the large string and rod puppets of Belgium, northern France, and Sicily. Acting out special versions of the great romantic legends of Europe such as *The Song of Roland*, the puppet plays are always full of knightly intrigues, adventures, and—most importantly—battles.

The hero of the puppet theater in Liège, Belgium, became popular in the early nineteenth century and is known as Tchantches. In Brussels, a similar character is called Woltje.

> In contrast to Charlemagne and his followers who preserve at least a modicum of princely speech, Chancet [Tchantches] always employs the native Waloon dialect.
> He is the popular spirit personified: although of humble birth, he is full of good humor and audacity; he is serious and gay by turns, and of a disconcerting familiarity. Chancet is the 'announcer' of the show, he fills in the interludes and picks up the corpses after a battle.[12]

During the last century, and to a limited extent even today, these Belgian puppet dramas were performed during the evenings in working class districts. Most often, the puppeteers were not professional entertainers and held other jobs during the day. Night after night, people from the neighborhood entered the simple basements or unadorned storerooms to watch the spectacles. Some complete play cycles required eight hundred elaborately carved and costumed figures. Usually, it would take several months of performances given serial fashion to complete the drama. Tchantches and Woltje were allowed to play important roles in the Trojan Wars, the legends of King Arthur, and biblical dramas as well as the adventures of Charlemagne and his court.

Normally, the dialogue and the narration were half read and half improvised, although certain conventions were observed. Audiences knew, for example, that large figures were stronger or more noble than

Large Belgian string and rod puppet warrior with metal helmet and sword dating from late nineteenth or early twentieth century. *Courtesy Alan G. Cook. (Photo by Alan G. Cook)*

small figures. In this way, Charlemagne might be nearly five feet tall, while a minor character might be less than eighteen inches high. Whenever a large figure representing a general, and six or seven small figures collided, often in midair, with a similar group, audience members understood that they were witnessing a titanic battle

between two great armies. Dead characters fell downstage—out of the way of the action—while those who were only wounded or knocked unconscious fell upstage where they could more conveniently rise again at the appropriate moments. Night fell when a sheet of metal was lowered, blocking off the light from the lamp used to illuminate the stage.[13]

One typical Liège puppet theater has been described in the following manner:

> . . . the auditorium . . . was six to eight meters long, three wide, two and a half high. Some benches of oak wood polished by use, were elevated in tiers placed diagonally in a single block, from the foot of the stage to the opposite wall.
>
> Above the narrow backstage entrance there was a sort of gallery which seemed made for puppets, but which served for the orchestra. The orchestra was composed ordinarily of a drum called 'caisse roulante' which was used for the marching of armies and for executing the tremoli accompanying all chivalric combats. On gala days, it was reinforced by a triangle and harmonica.
>
> The stage, elevated about one foot, was not without elegance, with curtains of black velvet spangled with tinsel stars of all shades. Save for this detail, the stage resembled that of any theatre. It was three meters long, one meter twenty-five centimeters high and one and a half meters deep.[14]

Most of the backdrops were painted on canvas. The exception was a painted wood backdrop that was used behind great battle scenes. The noise the puppets made as they clattered into it heightened the excitement of the battle scenes and the puppeteers did not need to worry about billowing or ripping fabric during the fighting. There were six or seven stock backgrounds and—as sometimes happened in the live theaters of the nineteenth century—the side wings were never changed. Some of the theaters were equipped with a stage floor that could be lifted up to reveal a tank of water. This make-believe ocean was the scene of surprisingly spectacular sea battles—complete with fireworks and beet juice blood.[15]

The heads and torsos of the Belgian rod and string figures were carved from wood. Although the legs and arms were articulated, the method of control with a single rod—called a *tringle*—attached to the head and two strings attached to the arms was not conducive to

Modern Sicilian rod puppet warrior made in 1970 for the "Little Theatre of Sicilian Puppets." *(Photo by David L. Young)*

Horse. From Sicilian rod puppet theater dating from late nineteenth or early twentieth century. Extremely rare figure. *Courtesy Alan G. Cook. (Photo by Alan G. Cook)*

graceful or subtle movement. The legs, which swung freely, produced a peculiar, awkward walk that was characteristic of these puppets. The best-known example of this form can still be seen in the Theatre Toone in Brussels. There are also some lesser known groups that continue to perform in Liège.

Today, there are four popular regional puppet heroes in Belgium. In addition to Tchantches and Woltje, who were mentioned earlier, there is de Neus, "the one with the long nose" from Antwerp, and in Ghent there is Pierke, or little Peter. Since 1938, there has been a concerted effort among Belgian puppeteers to create one Flemish national puppet hero. He is Tijl Uilenspiegel and, as of the time of this writing, he appears in about fifteen puppet theaters in different Flemish cities.

From the early eighteenth century until the beginning of this century, theaters similar to those in Belgium existed in Amiens, Lille, and Koubaix, which are all in northern France near the Belgian border. As with their Belgian counterparts, the French theaters were most popular during the ninteenth century and were essentially neighborhood entertainments. The feisty and talkative Lafleur was the hero of the puppet stage in Amiens. In Lille, the rough, fun-loving, but ultimately honorable favorite was Jacques, and in Koubaix, the hero

Ten-and-one-half-inch-high version of European Grand Turk, called The Terrible Turk. Made in the United States by Daniel Meader. Large head is hollow and two upper heads telescope down into it. *Courtesy Detroit Institute of Arts, Theatre Dept. (Photo by David L. Young)*

was the refined Bibilolo. In addition to the plays popular in the Belgian repertory, the puppeteers of northern France were quick to perform any material that suited their fancies. As a result, fairy tales, popular novels, and the stories of Aesop and La Fontaine were all performed in their theaters. Predictably, the most popular pieces were romantic tales of knightly adventure—most particularly, the adventures of Charlemagne.

Although the puppets of northern France were all designed along similar lines, there were some differences. Majorie Batchelder, for example, has observed that:

> The puppets of Lille were about thirty-six inches high, somewhat larger than those of Amiens. They differed also in having the head rod attached to an iron ring in the head, which allowed more flexible movement. The strings were attached to a wooden balance at the end of the *tringle*. An interesting fact about these puppets is that they were usually made by professional puppet makers, instead of by the showman himself.[16]

Considering the fact that during the late nineteenth century there were dozens of puppet theaters in operation at the same time, and that each of them used somewhere between three hundred and five hundred puppets, the existence of professional puppet makers in northern France is hardly surprising. Even without supplementing their income by the manufacture of toys or other sorts of wood craft, it is easy to imagine them earning a reasonable living.

While these spectacular, large, rod puppets enjoyed great popularity in Belgium and northern France, the beautiful figures undoubtedly found their most enthusiastic audiences in the cities and larger villages of Sicily. In the mid-1950s, it was usually assumed that this rod puppet form was almost extinct; but in recent years a large number of new theaters, which more or less follow the old traditions, have sprung up in Sicily as well as on the Italian mainland.

All of the countless episodes of the hundreds of plays in the Sicilian repertory are based on the *Orlando Furioso* written by the Italian Renaissance poet Ludovico Ariosto (1474–1533). The Orlando of the title is, of course, the Roland of the great French epic, *The Song of Roland,* which dates from the early twelfth century. The story concerns Roland's heroism as commander of Charlemagne's rear guard while traveling through the mountain passes of the Pyrenees. Through the treachery of Ganelon de Mayence, Roland is slain but Charlemagne is saved. In both *The Song of Roland* and *Orlando Furioso,* this basic plot is subject to considerable elaboration and

Nineteenth-century wooden pantin—or jumping-jack figure—of Columbine. *Courtesy Margo Lovelace. (Photo by David L. Young)*

expansion. Naturally, the story has been even further developed by the imaginative puppeteers of Sicily.

Bil Baird has said that the Sicilian rod puppet theatre:

> . . . obviously is the finest of puppet fare, and with improvements and additions by generations of puppeteers, it has become—and is today—a great, rich feast of giants, dragons, witches, ogres, eagles,

Eighteenth-century Venetian marionette of Commedia dell'Arte character, Brighella. *Courtesy Margo Lovelace. (Photo by David L. Young)*

magic swords, intrigues, transformations, heroics, betrayals, loves requited and unrequited and deaths, noble and ignoble. One complete version set down in the early nineteenth century began with Milone, the father of Orlando, and carried on through the death of Rinaldo, a journey which ran to three volumes and three thousand pages. To see every Orlando play from beginning to end would take more than three years of evenings in the theatre.[17]

Sicilian marionettes are large—often between three and four feet high—and are manipulated by rods. One rod is attached to each hand and another to the head. (Recall that in Belgium, the hands of the figures are usually controlled by strings rather than rods.) The figures are made to walk by allowing their legs to swing as a result of their own momentum. Some sets of figures are jointed at the knees, others are not. The puppets are often dressed in elaborate, handmade armor so that the total weight of a large figure often approaches one hundred pounds. As a result, the manipulation of these puppets requires enormous strength and endurance.

Nineteenth-century French carnival figures of traditional Punch and Judy characters. Carnival patrons would throw balls at figures to knock them over and win a prize. *Courtesy Alan G. Cook. (Photo by Alan G. Cook)*

34

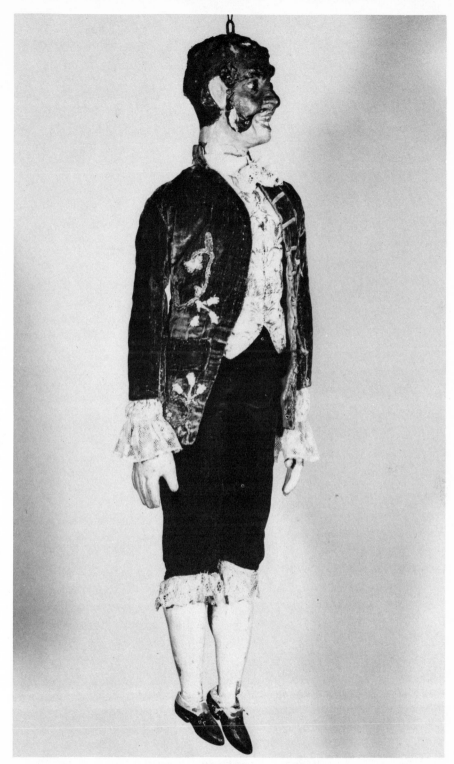

Venetian marionette wearing *Commedia* **mask. Date unknown.** *Courtesy Margo Lovelace. (Photo by David L. Young)*

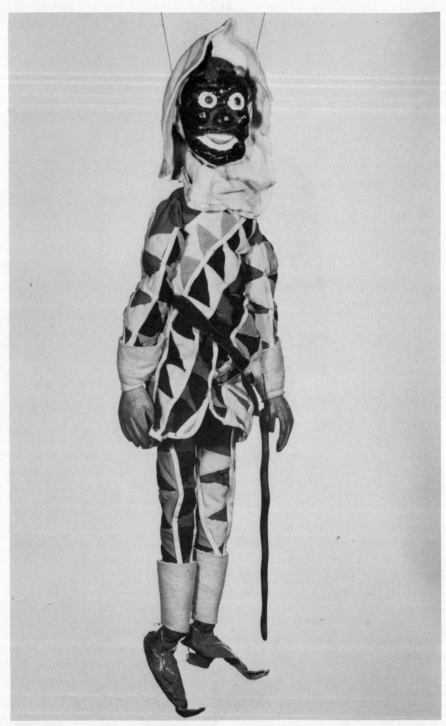

Eighteenth-century Venetian marionette of Commedia dell'Arte character, Arlequino. *Courtesy Margo Lovelace. (Photo by David L. Young)*

Largely because of the size of the figures and their crude method of manipulation, *The Opra dei Pupi*—as the Sicilian puppet theater is sometimes called—is by no means a subtle art. Its great attractions have always been spectacular battles in which the adversaries slash at each other with their swords and cut off one another's heads. Nonetheless, on occasion, the theater can create quieter moments of great depth and beauty.

Throughout Europe there are many puppets that have appeared or reappeared in only slightly altered form at different times and places. There are, for example, innumerable trick figures such as the French Mère Gigogne, who was popular from the seventeenth century until the end of the nineteenth. Her billowing costume hid numerous children who would appear with startling effect at the dramatic moment. Another popular trick puppet was the Grand Turk, who would come apart to form six smaller characters. One character came from his head, one from his body, one from each arm, and one from each leg. During the eighteenth century, string puppets in the likenesses of *Commedia dell'Arte* characters were quite popular in Venice and were known as Venetian marionettes. The Victoria and Albert Museum in London has a particularly fine collection of these figures along with an original theater.

There were—and are—many other traditions of folk puppetry in Europe as well as numerous regional puppet heroes and heroines. Beginning in Germany during the early sixteenth century, the legend of the brilliant but morally weak scientist, Dr. Faustus, became an extremely popular puppet play. Another well-known German tradition is the Hanneschen rod puppet theater of Cologne. The Hanneschen theater deals with the misadventures of the peasant Hanneschen and his relatives, his friends, his neighbors, his parents and grandparents, his girlfriend, a tavernkeeper, a serving maid, a schoolmaster, a provost, a policeman, a wine merchant, an architect, a prince, and some knights.[18] Hand puppets of the naïve silk-weaver, Guignol and his friend Gnafron, the soap maker of Lyons and the wiley Kasparek of Czechoslovakia achieved great popularity after 1850.

Unique localized forms of traditional puppetry can also be found, such as the *Kilim Arasi* style of Azervaijan in the USSR. Philpott describes this Russian type as "a kind of improvised puppet stage in which two men hold a folded carpet which conceals the operator of the hand puppets."[19] In Catalonia in notheastern Spain, an unusually large type of hand puppet is quite common. Three of the puppeteer's fingers are placed in the wooden head and shoulder piece while the thumb and small finger are inserted into cylindrical metal extenders to which are attached the puppet's hands. Traditional characters in the

Late nineteenth-century hand puppet of Guignol. The figure is twenty-two inches high with head and hands of carved wood. He wears a high, white collar, a red waistcoat, and a brown corduroy coat with silver buttons. *Courtesy Detroit Museum of Arts, Theatre Dept. (Photo by David L. Young)*

Catalan play include the heroine, Cristeta, Titella, Cristofel, la Cascarria, and a Devil. The central character is called Putxinellis, the Spanish Punch—a character that more than any other has become a symbol for folk puppet theater in the Western world.

Punch is the English name for a character type that has existed since the sixth century B.C. In the course of his long history he has acquired a large, prestigiously international family tree and has been played by masked actors, marionettes, and hand puppets. For over two thousand years he has, at one time or another, been a popular folk theater hero in almost every country in Europe.

Because his character has emerged as the product of so many artists in so many different places and times, there is no archetypal or perfect Punch. Nonetheless, it is possible to describe certain characteristics that all of his family share to a greater or lesser degree.

One of the most outstanding characteristics of Punch is his high-pitched, reedy voice—usually produced when the puppeteer speaks through a special instrument variously known as a swazzle, swatchel, call, slim, whistle, or pivetta. For most of his long history Punch was a hunchback. In most modern versions, this particular trait is eliminated, but the feisty antihero usually retains his long, hooked nose and matching chin. Punch has a comic street savvy and most often emerges victorious from his encounters with a dog, a doctor, a clown, a policeman, a hangman, and a devil. Punch's most famous adversary, however, is his tough, shrewish wife. In England and the United States she is most commonly known as Judy. A relatively new character, she first appeared in England during the seventeenth century. She was originally named Joan but in the late eighteenth century Punch was calling her "Joaney" and after 1825—perhaps because Joaney was difficult to say through a swazzle—she was commonly known as Judy.[20]

Punch's ancestry, on the other hand, can be traced back to the crude rustic farces variously called mimes, Atellan farces, and phylakes that were popular in ancient Greece and Rome between the sixth and third centuries B.C. Among the grotesquely masked and padded characters of these farces were Manducus, a crude country lout; Bucco, a sly and scheming comic slave; and Dossenus, a quick-witted hunchback. In both appearance and temperament, Punch bears a close family resemblance to all three of these characters.

These ancient farces, often violent and bawdy, were largely improvised from a loose collection of stock characters, situations, bits of stage business, and snatches of dialogue. The plays were probably first performed in open areas or on simple, wooden trestle stages that could be set up whenever and wherever crowds gathered in the ancient

Late nineteenth- or early twentieth-century Guignol stage with some characters.
Courtesy Everett and Ruth Kramer. (Photo by Alan G. Cook)

40

Pollack's Toy Theatres made from colored cardboard. Theaters such as this were popular as toys in nineteenth-century England. *Courtesy Alan G. Cook. (Photo by Alan G. Cook)*

world—in market places, in theaters, or at local celebrations. Records of such performances have survived in the form of pictures on certain ancient pottery vases.

The immediate descendants of Punch's Greek and Hellenistic ancestors can be found in scarcely altered form in the works of the Roman playwright Plautus, who lived in the second century B.C. In the enormous Roman theaters they gained a large following, often appearing before several thousand spectators at each performance. Such performances were widespread, because the Romans built theaters—and took their plays—throughout their enormous Empire, from the British Isles through Europe and the Middle East to North Africa. Undoubtedly, the memory of these popular characters lived long after the Roman conquerors became, in their turn, the conquered.

After the fall of Rome in the fifth century A.D., all theater artists were formally ostracized by the Catholic Church. Nonetheless, minstrels, court jesters, jongleurs, circus entertainers, illicit bands of roving

41

players—and puppeteers—preserved at least some of the popular theatrical traditions of the ancient world. These forms of popular entertainment eventually influenced and were influenced by the religious drama—which had its modest beginnings in the eleventh century, reached its height in the fourteenth century, and was rapidly fading in popularity by the time of Shakespeare's birth in 1564.

At about the same time that the religious drama was declining in popularity, a new form of masked and costumed drama developed in the Italian provinces. Like the ancient forms, these semi-improvised popular comedies—called *Commedia dell'Arte*—were based on stock characters in more or less standardized stage situations. The roster of *Commedia* characters included young lovers, a braggart warrior, clever servants, pseudolearned doctors, and greedy, lecherous old merchants. Among these characters was a curious figure with a high pointed hat and a huge hooked nose who became known as Pulcinella—and later, in France, as Polichinelle. By the time of the English Restoration in the 1660s, a puppet version of Pulcinella was appearing regularly in London as well as in many of the major cities in Europe. In England, his multisyllabic name was conveniently shortened to Punch and his character as a violent, squeaky-voiced comic antihero was almost complete. Whether or not Punch was a direct descendant of Pulcinella and the Greek and Roman stock characters is a matter for scholarly debate. But clearly, he represented a type that had amused European audiences for over two thousand years—and he was not about to leave the scene.

For the next one hundred years—well into the eighteenth century—Punch continued to build his popularity and extend his domain, appearing as a hand puppet, a string marionette, and even a live actor in all sorts of plays and entertainments throughout Europe. He appeared sometimes as hero, sometimes as antihero, in countless parodies of famous events and plays. During this period, Punch was most often portrayed as a weakling and a coward who lost most of his battles. Yet no matter how soundly he was beaten, he would always boast of victory—after his adversaries had left the stage.

It was not until the early nineteenth century that the tragical comedy of Punch and Judy began to appear in something like its present form. By this time, there were large numbers of Punch *professors,* as the showmen were called. In addition to their puppets, *professors* often worked with either a live dog or a monkey. They also relied heavily on their *bottlers,* who worked in front of the puppet booths to collect money, interpret the speech of the puppet characters for the audience, and prevent the crowds from annoying the puppeteer.

There are a number of standard characters in the Punch and Judy

Catalan hand puppet made in approximately 1890. It was used until 1965 by Jaime Anglés of Barcelona. *Courtesy Alan G. Cook. (Photo by Alan G. Cook)*

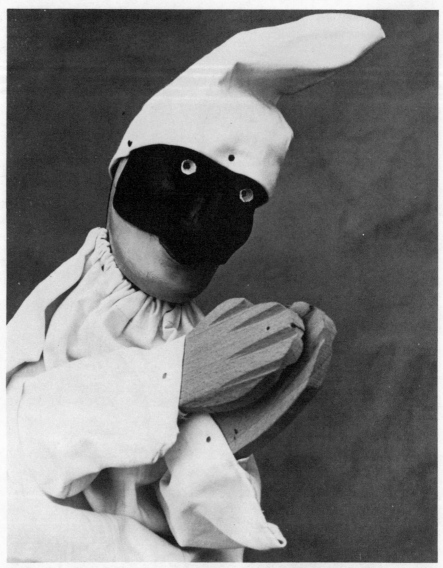

Modern Pulcinella hand puppet from Rome. *Courtesy Alan G. Cook. (Photo by Alan G. Cook)*

performances that different *professors* varied to suit their individual needs and tastes. In addition to Toby, the dog, the traditional puppet cast included Toby's owner, Punch, Judy, the baby, a servant, a doctor, a horse, a clown named Joey, a policeman, a hangman named Jack Ketch, and either a devil or an alligator.

One of the characteristics of the Punch and Judy shows—as with much popular theater—is that, in order to make a living, the performers had to travel to their audiences rather than relying on their audiences to come to them. As a result, the stages were always light and portable and were usually simply constructed, canvas covered, wooden frames. If necessary, light was provided by a lantern placed on one or both sides of the playing area.

The plot outline of a typical, traditional Punch and Judy play takes the following form. At the beginning of the play, Punch introduces himself and the play to the audience. Then, he calls for his wife, Judy. Instead of Judy, he encounters his neighbor's vicious dog, Toby. Punch tries to befriend the animal but is not very successful. The dog bites Punch's nose and then exits in order to look for his master. While Punch is nursing his hurt pride and wounded nose, Toby's owner enters and, after some broad slapstick byplay, Punch takes his revenge and knocks the owner senseless. Next, Punch calls to Judy and, after some flattery, she agrees to come upstairs. After some comic banter, Judy tells her husband that she has to go out for awhile. She brings in Baby, and tells Punch to take care of "it." Punch tries to get Baby to go to sleep but Baby won't and in a famous and—for many modern audiences—controversial scene, Punch throws Baby out the window.

German wooden Punch and Judy set made as toys during the late nineteenth century. *Author's collection. (Photo by David L. Young)*

German wooden Punch, Judy, with dog, Toby. *Courtesy Frank Paris (Photo by Alan G. Cook)*

Judy returns, misses Baby, and fights with Punch. The slapstick skill with which Punch killed Judy was a point of great pride with the traditional *professors*. (It is worth noting that modern American Punch and Judy performers tend to dispense with all of the killing, while many English performers tend to leave it in—with equally satisfactory results.) In any event, after his battle with Judy, Punch rests for awhile, sometimes talking to his horse. When the horse leaves, a doctor enters to see Judy, but he soon begins to take a professional interest in Punch. He prescribes some unpleasant medicine in the form of a few taps with the slapstick, but the clever Punch outwits the doctor and kills him. In celebration, Punch sings a song—off-key and a little too loudly. At this point, a neighbor's servant enters and asks Punch not to make so much noise. Until this century, the servant was usually black. But no matter what his color, he is always stupid, rather pompous, and scarcely a match for the wily Punch who eventually kills him. As the servant expires, Punch's best friend, Joey the clown, enters to warn Punch that a visitor is about to arrive. There follows an elaborate piece of traditional stage business: Punch counts bodies

46

while Joey keeps confusing the process by changing the position of the puppets. Punch's frantic miscounting never fails to amuse the audience. Joey exits just before the arrival of the Policeman, who is both a genuine authority figure and a typical example of the classical, braggart warrior. Punch finally seems to have met his just reward as the Policeman drags him off to jail. When Jack Ketch, the hangman, arrives and begins to set up the gallows, Punch tries to persuade the hangman to let him go and, in another controversial scene, he manages to hang the hangman. On the verge of freedom, Punch encounters either the alligator who threatens to eat him, or the devil, who offers to drag him into the nether world. But Punch generally manages to emerge victorious and concludes the play with a little song.

If, after the first one or two scenes of the play were completed, the show had failed to attract a decent crowd, the puppeteer would simply abbreviate his show, pack up his theater, and move it to a more likely spot. Only if the crowds were large, appreciative, and most importantly, generous, would he bother to perform the entire play. Punch and Judy *professors* were remarkably adept at finding the most profitable pitches—places to perform—in the cities and resort areas of Europe and the British Isles.

In an article about Punch in the December 1972 issue of *The Saturday Review,* Muriel Broadman Lobl referred to him as "the quintessential puppet of Western civilization."[21] With his many relatives throughout the world: Kasper in Germany, Jan Klassen in the Netherlands, Master Jakel in Denmark; in Hungary, Vitez Lazlo, Vasilache in Rumania and, perhaps, Karagoz of Greece, North Africa, and the Middle East, Punch amply deserves this impressive title.

Some people believe that the future of Punch is in doubt, that he is evolving into a polite—or worse, cute—entertainment performed exclusively for children. His true home, however, is in the busy backstreets and crowded plazas and squares of the Western world's great cities. And, for as long as people need to laugh, there will be a place for Punch—the world's smallest antihero. Without question, he represents the longest-lived and most vigorous tradition of folk puppetry that Europe has ever known.

NOTES

1. George Speaight, *Punch and Judy: A History.* (Boston: Plays, Inc., 1970), pp. 16–17.
2. Bil Baird, *The Art of the Puppet* (New York: Macmillan, 1965), p. 65.
3. Marjorie Batchelder, *Rod Puppets and the Human Theatre* (Columbus: Ohio Univ. Press, 1947), p. 72.

4. Baird, *The Art of the Puppet*, p. 64.
5. Batchelder, *Rod Puppets and The Human Theatre*, p. 75.
6. Ibid., p. 125.
7. A. R. Philpott, *Dictionary of Puppetry* (Boston: Plays, Inc., 1969), p. 125.
8. G. A. d'Agnel, and Leopold Dor, *Noël en Provençe* (Paris, 1972), quoted in Batchelder, *Rod Puppets and the Human Theatre*, p. 143.
9. Max Von Boehn, *Puppets and Automata* (New York: Dover, 1972), p. 11.
10. Gunter Bohmer, *The Wonderful World of Puppets*. (Boston: Plays, Inc., 1969), pp. 41–43.
11. Philpott, *Dictionary of Puppetry*, p. 92.
12. Batchelder, *Rod Puppets and the Human Theatre*, p. 154.
13. Ibid., p. 154.
14. R. Warsage, *Histoire du Célèbre Théâtre Liègeois de Marionettes* (Brussels: 1905), trans. and adapted in Batchelder, p. 152.
15. Batchelder, *Rod Puppets and the Human Theatre*, p. 152.
16. Ibid., p. 157.
17. Baird, *Art of the Puppet*, p. 119.
18. Batchelder, *Rod Puppets and the Human Theatre*, p. 137.
19. Philpott, *Dictionary of Puppetry*, p. 130.
20. Speaight, *Punch and Judy: A History*, p. 85.
21. Muriel Broadman Lobl, "Punch," *The Saturday Review* (December 1972), p. 37.

2

Shadow Puppets of Greece, Turkey, the Middle East, and North Africa

Although puppet theaters throughout the Middle East have used hand and string puppets for centuries, by far the most widespread form has been the shadow puppet. Four major scholars in the field, Sabri Esat Siyavusgil, Metin Änd, Cevedet Kudret, and Jacob Landau subscribe to the belief that the Middle Eastern shadow theater developed from similar but older traditions in Indonesia, China, and India. However, the German expert, Max Von Boehn, has written that the unique shadow theater form that developed in the Middle East originated in Egypt and Turkey during the eleventh and twelfth centuries A.D. It is possible that the shadow puppets became popular because they circumvented the orthodox Moslem prohibition against the use of human effigies. Ostensibly, the thin camel or donkey leather from which the figures were made was carefully and intricately pierced in order to destroy any possible illusion of life. It is probably worth noting that such an explanation is subject to argument, particularly since Moslem paintings have always commonly included human portraits. In any event, as the shadow show grew in popularity, many individual puppeteers throughout Asia Minor and North Africa took pains to create their own characters, stories, and styles of performance. But eventually, two puppet characters emerged to dominate the shadow screens of Greece, Turkey, the Middle East, and North Africa.

According to a popular legend, the major characters were modeled after two Turkish laborers named Karagöz and Hacivad who lived during the fourteenth century. While working on the construction site of a new mosque at Bursa, their continual comic arguments distracted

Modern Turkish miniature of Karagoz, chief character in the shadow plays of Greece, Turkey, North Africa, and the Middle East. He always has a rounded beard and wears a huge turban to hide his bald head. His name means "dark eye." *Author's collection. (Photo by David L. Young)*

the other workers and brought progress on the project to a virtual halt. When the problem was brought to the attention of the sultan, he became enraged and ordered the immediate execution of the two lively workers. But soon after their death, the sultan grew despondent over his hasty decision. In order to lift the spirits of the unhappy monarch, a Turkish master puppeteer named Sheik Kusteri made two shadow figures of Karagöz and Hacivad. His performance, which cleverly

Modern Turkish miniature of Karagoz's friend, Hacivad, who always has a slightly turned-up, pointed beard. *Author's collection. (Photo by David L. Young)*

imitated the voices and mannerisms of the workmen, delighted the sultan and was the beginning of the tradition of Karagöz performances. For centuries, in honor of his contribution, the name of Sheik Kusteri was worked into the songs and dialogues of the Turkish plays.

However true or untrue this legend may be, it seems likely that after Egypt was annexed as a part of the Ottoman Empire in 1517, regional shadow theaters were increasingly influenced by the extremely

Modern Turkish miniature of a young dancing girl. *Courtesy Thomas Goodrich. (Photo by David L. Young)*

popular Turkish models. The form retained its essentially Turkish characteristics wherever it went, but because nomadic Gypsy tribes were a significant factor in transporting the tradition to new areas, there were also strong Gypsy elements in the plays. In fact, in some areas, Karagöz himself was portrayed as a Gypsy rather than as a Turk. Today, with some more or less minor differences, the shadow

Modern Turkish miniature of a wealthy and heavily veiled woman. *Courtesy Thomas Goodrich. (Photo by David L. Young)*

puppet traditions of Greece, North Africa, Turkey, and the Middle East closely resemble one another.

From the seventeenth century through the first decade of the twentieth century, Karagöz—called Karaghiozis in Greece—became the leading player in the shadow theaters of these regions. Along with his friend, Hacivad—called Aiwaz in the Arab countries—he played

Modern Turkish miniature of a pregnant young woman. *Courtesy Thomas Goodrich. (Photo by David L. Young)*

before an almost endless variety of audiences that included royal princes, middle class families, and uneducated workers. The Karagöz puppeteers, called *hayaldji* or *karagötsci* in Turkey, usually worked from scenarios rather than from finished scripts. In this way, they could easily adapt a single story line to the tastes of different spectators. Crude humor was an important ingredient in some of the performances, but not in others. This ability to adapt to the tastes of

Modern Turkish miniature of Tiryaki, the opium eater, who is never without his pipe and fan. *Courtesy Thomas Goodrich. (Photo by David L. Young)*

his audiences was probably a vital factor in any *hayaldji*'s continued success.

All performances had a clearly identifiable form that included four distinct sections.

The first part was an *Introduction* that began to the accompaniment of a simple reed instrument called a *nareke*. The decorative leather ornaments that adorned the screen while the audience was getting seated were removed and Hacivad entered singing. In the lyrics, materialistic values were unfavorably compared to the search for ultimate spiritual truths. At the end of the song, Hacivad greeted the audience and immediately began to wish aloud for a cultured and brilliant companion—someone, as he saw it, like himself. Then he began to yell for Karagöz to come and join him. Between yells, he heaped abuse on his "friend," characterizing him as crude, boorish, and uneducated. Finally, Karagöz, who had been secretly watching, could take it no longer. He leapt from his hiding place and attacked the surprised Hacivad, who escaped with only minor wounds to his body but major damage to his oversized ego. While Karagöz was busy justifying his attack to the audience, a somewhat contrite Hacivad returned and the *Dialogue*—or second part of the performance—began.

In this section, Hacivad tried to sustain an intellectual discussion with Karagöz. But Karagöz either could not or, more probably, would not understand him. They bantered back and forth for a while, each making jokes at the expense of the other. Most puppeteers were careful to insert some topical humor and local references into this section. According to tradition, the more expert the performer, the longer he could keep an audience involved in the *Dialogue*. Sooner or later, however, Karagöz lost his temper and, once again, Hacivad was beaten off the stage.

At this point, the *Action* of the play began. This part of the performance sometimes took the form of a more or less involved story complete with problems, complications, and solutions. On other occasions, the section resembled a revue. That is, various comic bits were shown in sequence with little or no unifying plot or theme.

Finally, there was a brief *Epilogue* in which Hacivad and Karagöz returned for one last argument. Hacivad was pummeled yet again, Karagöz said his goodbyes to the audience, and the performance was over.

Like the popular Italian *Commedia dell'Arte* scenarios of the sixteenth through eighteenth centuries, these plays included a number of stock characters in a wide variety of situations. Only Karagöz—which means "dark eye" in Turkish—and his pretentious, dramatic foil, Hacivad, appeared in every play.

During the *Introduction, Dialogue,* and *Epilogue* Karagöz sported a rounded beard and wore the traditional clothing of a middle class Turk, complete with an oversized turban. But during the *Action* of the play he was likely to appear in almost any kind of costume: baker, boatman, physician, or merchant. In one play, he went so far as to disguise himself as a woman. To his conservative Moslem audience, this was particularly outrageous behavior.

Like his Western counterpart, Punch, Karagöz was a hunchback.

For many centuries, both in Europe and the Middle East, clowns were traditionally misshapen.

Karagöz was basically a simple peasant with a natural, if well-disguised, moral sensibility. He was also blessed with a crude and ready wit. Nonetheless, he was constantly the target of everyone else's jokes and pranks. Like many folk clowns, he was a chronic bumbler with a finely honed instinct for somehow turning the worst of situations to his own advantage.

Puppets representing Karagöz always had at least two and sometimes three special features. First, the turban was constructed so that it could be made to slip off the puppet's head at appropriate moments. Second, one of the arms was abnormally long so that Karagöz's gestures could have additional expressiveness. Third, Karagöz was often endowed with an enormous phallus that was used in broadly farcical ways. For example, in one popular play Karagöz is shown lying unconscious in the street with his phallus pointing skyward. Suddenly, some brigands ride up, dismount, tie their horses to it, and exit.

In the *Prologue, Dialogue,* and *Epilogue* Hacivad was dressed in much the same manner as Karagöz. But since he wore a pointed, as opposed to Karagöz's rounded, beard it was always easy to tell them apart. In keeping with his inflated self-image, Hacivad would rarely stoop to disguise himself. His speech was filled with ostensibly learned language and sprinkled with amusingly misquoted phrases from a wide diversity of religious and philosophical sources. In contrast, his knowledge of music was amazingly extensive and precise. He is remembered chiefly because he was always hilariously pompous and conceited.

One of the more popular characters in the plays was Celebi. He was a likeable dandy who could easily afford his expensive tastes. He was well dressed, well educated, philanthropic, and a patron of the arts. Like many of the puppet cast, he normally held at least one symbol of his status or identity. In his case, this was likely to be a fly swatter, silk handkerchief, or tulip—signs of his idleness and high social status.

All of the women and girls in the plays were called *zenna*. This term applied to all imaginable types and nationalities including slaves, nurses, wealthy women, middle class women, Arabs, Turks, Europeans, innocent young girls, and prostitutes. Predictably, the prostitute, with her many lovers, vicious temper, and wily manner, was often the most important female character. Karagöz's shrewish wife ran a close second.

Tiryaki, the opium addict—Afyani in the Arab performances—always held his pipe in one hand and a fan in the other. He was

Modern Turkish miniature of a dervish or holy man who holds a string of prayer beads. *Courtesy Thomas Goodrich. (Photo by David L. Young)*

hunchbacked like Karagöz and only slightly less pretentious than Hacivad. Because of his drug habit, he had a tendency to fall asleep at odd moments, often in the middle of a conversation or argument. Upon awakening, he would become highly energetic for a few moments and then he would quickly fall asleep once again. Under the influence of his drug, he often became amazingly bold and undertook incredible feats of daring. But before he got very far, the drug would wear off and he would fall asleep on the spot—no matter where he was or what he was doing—always snoring loudly. He was usually a tragicomic figure on the fringes of the play's central action.

With a fez on his head and a sack on his back, this plainly dressed figure is clearly a Turkish peasant. A modern Turkish miniature. *Courtesy Thomas Goodrich. (Photo by David L. Young)*

Beberuhi was a dwarf and a simpleton. Despite a certain childlike naiveté, he was hardly ever presented sympathetically. With his huge appetite and his tendency to engage in long-winded, senseless monologues, he was either viciously beaten by Karagöz or frightened away by the arrival of the fierce Albanian, Tuzus Deli Bekir.

This character would bluster on to the scene toward the end of the play carrying a jug of wine in one hand and a pistol, rifle, or sword in the

Negroes in the Turkish shadow plays are usually either servants, as shown here, or musicians. A modern Turkish miniature. *Courtesy Thomas Goodrich. Photo by David L. Young)*

other. He resolved all of the remaining dramatic conflicts whether they were physical, legal, or moral. Although he was a tough and uninhibited warrior, he was never a bully, and his settlements, which were both just and compassionate, provided entirely suitable happy endings to the plays. In his book *The Turkish Theatre*, Nicholas Martinovitch wrote that Tuzus Deli Bekir was sometimes presented as a satire on the Turkish Janissaries—the militia. Other scholars, noting that the Ottoman government did not tolerate criticism, believe that

Heavily armed figure with a scimitar and sword represents one of a number of warlike tribesmen from Asia Minor. Modern Turkish miniature. *Courtesy Thomas Goodrich. (Photo by David L. Young)*

any political satire or parody directed toward the government agencies could only have been of the mildest sort.

In addition to the major characters, there were always a number of minor figures in the shadow plays. These included, but were not limited to, the Persian, the European, the Jew, the Arab, and various tribesmen from Asia Minor. Each of these characters could be identified by his distinctive appearance. For example, Europeans were

61

recognizable because of their Western style clothing. Arabs wore their traditional headgear, and Jews always appeared with sacks on their backs. The identification of other minor characters required some knowledge of Middle Eastern costume as well as a familiarity with the traditions of Karagöz theater.

The best, old, Middle Eastern shadow figures are made from translucent donkey or camel skin. This is carefully cut and dyed so that the shadows, which are thrown onto the screen, resemble, from the audience's point of view, an animated stained glass window. Sometimes a puppeteer manipulated all of the figures himself, sometimes he employed assistants. One of his helpers accompanied the show on the *nareke* and handed the performer the puppets as he needed them. The puppeteer sat behind a muslin or oiled paper screen pressing and manipulating the puppets against it with a number of thin rods that fitted into sockets on the puppets. These rods were not permanently attached to the figures in any way, so that whenever the puppeteer wished to change puppets, he had only to remove one puppet from the rods and pick up another. By keeping these rods perpendicular to the plane of the screen and placing the light source between himself and the screen, the puppeteer made his control rods and himself virtually invisible to the audience.

The puppets were usually from twelve to sixteen inches high, although some were as small as seven inches and others were as large as forty inches. Normally, each puppet had only three or four joints. There was one at the waist, a second and third at each knee, and a fourth at one of the elbows. On occasion, both elbows were jointed. Certain trick figures were made with additional joints. The joints were made by passing a gut cord through the pieces to be joined and then knotting it at both ends.

The Greek Kharaghiosis was wiser, more witty, and less of a clown than his Turkish brother. Greek figures were usually somewhat larger than the Turkish and, as a result, were presented on slightly larger screens. The stories, characters, and individual episodes, however, were all remarkably similar to their Turkish counterparts.

Unfortunately, the traditional theater of Karagöz is a dying art. There are only a handful of expert showmen left in the world. As a result, genuine professional or old puppets are extremely difficult to find for sale. However, in the major market places and bazaars of Greece, Turkey, North Africa, and the Middle East, one can still find craftsmen who make and sell high quality reproductions. A somewhat greater number make and market six- or seven-inch-high miniature reproductions of the once well-known characters. Although these are not suitable for performance since they are too small and lack holes for the manipulation rods, the best of them are made in the traditional manner and are worth the usually reasonable prices that are asked. The worst are hastily cut from cardboard and crudely painted with water colors or poster paints. They are the final sad remnants of a once vigorous tradition.

3

Puppets in Sub-Sahara Africa

Sub-Sahara Africa is, without question, a vast and significant source for a large variety of ritual masks, figurines, and dolls. The art of puppetry, however, has apparently never been as prominent in this region as it has in some other areas of the world. Nonetheless, on the basis of museum collections as well as from a very few eyewitness accounts, it seems likely that puppets and puppet performances existed—and in some cases still exist—among such peoples as the Ibo, Ibibio, Bozo, Somono, Haoussas, Pangwe, and Bambara. Because many of the performances are or were part of highly secret tribal rituals, and because of a simple lack of reliable information, very little is known concerning the puppetry of sub-Sahara Africa.

P. Amaury Talbot, in *Life in Southern Nigeria*, has described in detail the performance of an Ibibio puppet play that he and his wife saw during the first quarter of this century. The performance, which Talbot says was called the Akan play, had twenty characters and was performed in an open, sandy area. The puppeteers were concealed from the spectators by means of blankets that were carefully sewn together and suspended from wooden rails. This "theater" was about twenty feet long and six feet wide. Special "beaters" stood in front of the theater and continually struck the front curtain in order to help conceal the backstage movement of the puppeteers. The performance itself was evidently a combination of "live" actors and puppeteers. The puppeteers spoke through a special squeaker—various types of which are common among puppeteers in all parts of the world—in order to create the puppets' voices. This version of it was "a small tube made from corn-stalk covered with the membrane taken from beneath a bat's wing."[1] Talbot does not describe the specific subject matter of

Ibibio puppet activated by rods and strings. *Courtesy Museum of Cultural History, UCLA. (Photo by Alan G. Cook)*

the play except to note that it dealt with a series of topical events drawn from tribal culture. It included scenes of domestic life as well as a number of satirical references to the prevailing systems of tribal and colonial government.

As is common in folk puppet plays, there was evidently a good deal of bawdiness, which Talbot carefully avoids examining.

The rest of the play is indescribeable. I am happy to say that this is the only occasion on which we have encountered an instance of real vulgarity among primitive African peoples. Up till now, even when touching on subjects usually avoided by Europeans on account of difficulty of treatment, the perfect simplicity of manner and purpose

65

with which such were mentioned or explained robbed them of possible offence. In this one case, most unfortunately, inexcusable and irrelevant coarseness showed itself, naked and unashamed, and we could not but wonder as to the influence to which such innovation was due.[2]

Despite his obvious embarrassment concerning its subject matter, Talbot noted that the play had been rehearsed with great care and precision. Rehearsals took place at night and intricate precautions were taken to assure that no woman ever learned the secret of how the puppets were operated. If, during a performance, a puppet was mishandled in such a way that its mechanics were revealed to the audience, the whole company was likely to be slain by the spectators. At the very least, the offending puppeteer would be killed.[3]

Talbot also makes a brief reference to performances called *Ekkbo Akpara*, which Ibibio shamans performed in marketplaces or town squares. The theater was a palm stem supported by two notched stakes. Small fetishes were balanced on the palm stem and made to dance and talk in time to the increasingly rapid rhythms of tom-toms. The performance is not described in detail but the resulting illusion was evidently quite impressive. Talbot finds it necessary to discuss the performance with reference to the "recent experiments in France, which seem to prove that certain people have the power of influencing objects without touching them, as well as the telekinetic phenomena at spiritualistic seances."[4]

In his brief but important article, "African Puppets," which appeared in a 1965 issue of *World Theatre,* Jacques Chenais has described two puppet shows that he saw in West Africa. Chenais characterizes the performances among the Bozo and Somono fishermen in southwestern Mali as "rod puppet theatres of exceptional dramatic intensity."[5] The shows often satirized local traditions, customs, and power structures. Other performances took the form of dramatized eulogies in which the principal characters were praised for their many virtues. Old folk stories were told and retold with ever-increasing dramatic embellishment in the form of fantastic deeds and great feats of magic. The identities of the puppeteers were closely guarded secrets—partially in order to enhance the mystic aura of the performances and partially to protect the puppeteers from the objects of their satire.

Chenais witnessed a very different type of puppet show among the Haoussas people at Zinder in southern Niger. The most important person in the six-member puppet troupe was the *dabola*, or puppeteer. The puppets were called *dabo-dabo*. There was also a second

Indian shadow figure from Karnatak. Control rod running up through the center of the puppet has been removed. *Author's collection. (Photo by David L. Young)*

This Mére Gigogne figure is probably well over one hundred years old and has been recostumed several times. At the proper dramatic moment, "dozens" of children would appear from beneath her costume. *Author's collection. (Photo by David L. Young)*

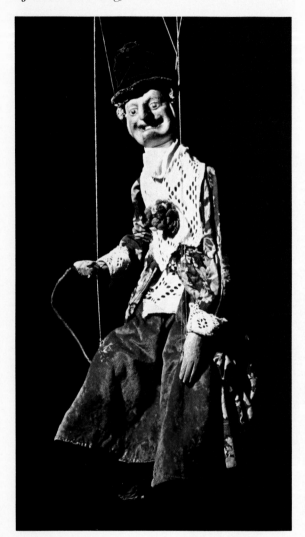

Turkish shadow figure of Karagöz disguised as a woman. *Courtesy Marg Lovelace. (Photo by David L. Young)*

Modern Chinese hand puppet from Taiwan. *Courtesy Suzanne Gabig. (Photo by David L. Young)*

Eighteenth-century Venetian hand puppet of Pantalone, with movable eyes and jaw. *Courtesy the Detroit Museum of Arts, Theatre Department. (Photo by David L. Young)*

***Wayang klitik*, carved wood figure with leather arms from Java. Cour** *Margo Lovelace. (Photo by David L. Young)*

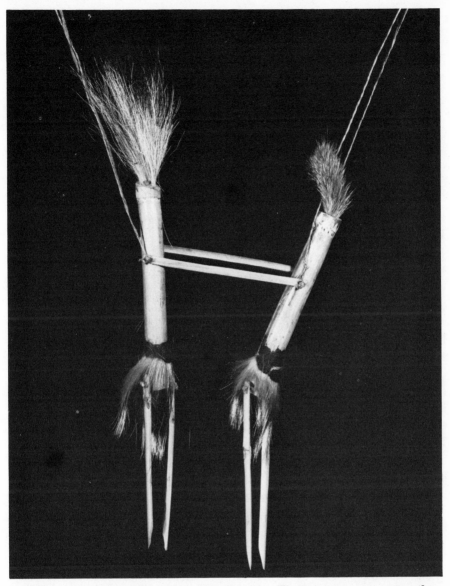

Tulukutu **type puppet from Western Zambia. The puppeteer operates these "jigging" figures with his feet.** *Courtesy Margo Lovelace. (Photo by David L. Young)*

individual who served as a kind of master of ceremonies and a third, whom Chenais calls "the interpreter," whose function was to translate the unintelligible, high-pitched puppet voices into words that the members of the audience could understand. There were also three drummers, one of whom, Chenais says, was a child.

Chenais's comments on the structure of the Haoussas puppet theater, although interesting, are probably not quite as clear as they could be:

> The puppeteer chooses his site with extreme care. After making a barrier of sand 20 centimetres high and about a metre long, he drives a stick into the ground to the height of a man in a squatting position, roughly one metre to the rear of the barrier; having placed the bags containing the puppets in their prescribed position, he sits down tailorwise beside the stick; he then envelops both himself and his material in a large 'boubou' with a hole at its centre.[6]

During performances, the puppeteer speaks through yet another type of squeaker. In contrast to the one used by the Ibibio, the Haoussas type is very similar to the traditional *swazzle* used by English Punch and Judy showmen. Two small silver plates are bound loosely together and held against the roof of the puppeteer's mouth. Since the resulting high-pitched sounds are very nearly unintelligible, the presence of the interpreter is completely justified.

The drummers sit behind the action and begin by playing an introduction to the actual performance. The sound of the drums serves as an announcement to all those in the area that the show is about to begin. During these preliminaries, the interpreter places a number of obscene figures on top of the sand barrier in order to serve as a symbolic separation between the members of the audience and the theater. Chenais says that another reason for the presence of these figures is to offer a deliberate challenge to the Moslem priests of the area. In keeping with the orthodox precepts of Islam, the priests oppose any representation of human images and often take elaborate measures to prevent the puppeteers from performing.

The figures themselves are glove puppets with cotton heads and bodies.

> Some are extremely lifelike and have undoubtedly been inherited; the others, on the contrary, verge on the abstract and are very certainly the puppeteer's own handiwork. The face, notably, is merely suggested by a section of the printed pattern, the general outline is stylized and conventional, attributes of sex are unmistakable.[7]

There is a photograph of two such puppets from Chenais's private collection included with his article. Unfortunately, Chenais does not describe the stories or plots of any of the several plays that he saw among the Haoussas.

Another type of African puppet can be found in the Barotse Province

Merekun **puppet of the Bambara tribe in Mali. One string activates the left and another the right arm of this female figure.** *Courtesy Alan G. Cook. (Photo by Alan G. Cook)*

in western Zambia. Known as *tulu-kutu*, the puppet is really two small wooden figures that are about nine inches high and share a single pair of arms. The puppeteer sits on the ground with a string from each puppet looped around his two big toes. In this fashion, a slight movement of the puppeteer's feet causes the puppets to dance. Other similar puppets have been observed among the Mbuda, Lubala,

Sub-Sahara Africa, specific origin unknown. One arm of each of the figures moved as the whole scene was carried aloft on a stick. *Courtesy Alan G. Cook. (Photo by Alan G. Cook)*

Chokwe, and Luchazi tribes. There is some speculation that such figures may be of European rather than native African origin.[8]

Among the Bambara people in Mali, figures called *merekun* are used by masked dancers disguised as birds. The dancer/actor/puppeteer thrusts the figure through his palm-fibered costume and makes it speak in a high falsetto voice. Photographs of these figures appear in *Sculpture of Black Africa: The Paul Dishman Collection* by Roy Sieber and Arnold Rubin,[9] and Robert Goldwater's *Bambara Sculpture from the Western Sudan*.[10] There are two *merekun* in the collection of the Museum of Primitive Art in New York City. One of these is a particularly fine specimen that is completely costumed and stands over two feet high.

Another type of puppet used by Bambara storytellers is described and illustrated in Günter Böhmer's *The Wonderful World of Puppets*.[11] Böhmer says, "The figures have elongated angular heads and deep-set eyes, in which bits of mirror have been inserted, with metal bands and helmet-like head and brow shields. Their throats end in sticks which thicken to form their chest and are than so secured to the operating rods that they can see-saw as the narrator tells his story."[12]

It is likely that there were and are many more types of puppets in sub-Sahara Africa than scholarly research has yet revealed. But since many kinds of puppetry are cloaked in secrecy and African puppets often bear little relationship to Western concepts of how puppets should look, clear, unequivocal identification of many figures is often difficult to obtain. It would not be surprising to learn that many of the objects that are labeled figures and fetishes in the museums of the world were, in fact, used as puppets. Perhaps, as more is learned about African culture, new information will emerge concerning the folk art and traditions of African puppetry.

NOTES

1. P. Amaury Talbot, *Life in Southern Nigeria* (New York: Barnes and Noble, 1967), p. 77.
2. Ibid., p. 78.
3. Ibid., p. 79.
4. Ibid., p. 72.
5. Jacques Chesnais, "Marionnettes Africaines," *World Theatre* vol. 14, no. 5 (Sept. 1965), p. 448.
6. Ibid., p. 450.
7. Ibid., pp. 450–51.
8. A. R. Philpott, *Dictionary of Puppetry* (Boston: Plays, Inc., 1969), p. 267.
9. Roy Sieber and Arnold Rubin, *Sculpture of Black Africa: The Paul Dishman Collection* (Los Angeles: L.A. County Museum of Art, 1968), p. 40.
10. Robert Goldwater, *Bambara Sculpture from the Western Sudan* (New York: University Publishers, 1960), pp. 34–35.
11. Günter Böhmer, *The Wonderful World of Puppets*. Trans. Gerald Morice. (Boston: Plays, Inc., 1969), p. 106.
12. Ibid., p. 107.

4

India and Sri Lanka
The Cradle of Puppetry

INDIA

Many experts are convinced that puppetry is the oldest form of popular theater in India. In order to support this belief, they point out that the term *sutradhara* or threadholder was the term for the director or the stage manager in the live, classical Sanskrit theater of ancient India (A.D. 100–1000). They reason that this use of terminology derived from the puppet theater is evidence that puppetry preceded the live theater in India. It is also widely believed that in ancient times severe penalties were imposed on any individual who inpersonated someone of another caste—but that the puppeteers grew in popularity largely because they were not restricted in this way.[1]

Other scholars are persuaded that India has had its live actors for thousands of years—and that any penalties imposed on performers were as likely a result of the caprice of local rulers as of orthodox religious principles. They also note that the use of the term *sutradhara* to mean director or stage manager did not first occur until long after the golden age of Sanskrit drama in the fifth century A.D.

Whatever the truth may be, it is certain that India's diverse cultures have developed a rich variety of fascinating styles of string, rod, shadow, and hand puppets.

According to Mrs. Meher Contractor, there are large numbers of traditional and folk puppets that still survive in India. These include: (1) string puppets, or *kathputlis*, of Rajasthan; (2) string puppets of Orissa; (3) rod puppets from Bengal; (4) combination rod and string

A *Kathputli* figure from the state of Rajasthan in Northern India. When properly manipulated, this twenty-three-inch-high figure performs juggler's tricks with the wooden ball. *Author's collection. (Photo by David L. Young)*

puppets of Tanjore, Madras, and Andhra; (5) shadow puppets of Orissa, Malabar, Andhra, and Karnatak; and (6) glove puppets from Madras, Kerala, and Malabar.[2] In addition, there are the famed *yakshagana* puppets of India's southeast coast, which are no longer extant.

Many of the puppet dramas of India and the other nations of Asia are strongly based on the two major Indian, Hindu epics, the *Ramayana* and the *Mahabharata*. The *Ramayana* is concerned with the lives and exciting adventures of Ramachandra and his wife Sita while the *Mahabharata* deals with a series of conflicts between two great families, the noble Pandavas and their cousins and enemies, the evil Kauravas.

The oldest style of string puppetry in India is found in the northern state of Rajasthan. According to an ancient legend, the first Rajasthani puppeteer was born out of the mouth of Brahma, the creator. Given this tradition of divine origin, it is not surprising that, for hundreds of years, the puppeteers of Rajasthan have devoted immeasurable time and skill to the service of their art. Rajasthani puppeteers trace their historical descent from the court actors and dancers known as *bhats*, a name derived from Bharata, the legendary founder of the arts of music and dance in India. Their beautifully balanced yet mechanically uncomplicated puppets are called *kathputli*. According to J. Tilakasiri, author of *The Puppet Theatre of Asia*:

These performers who share the title *nats* or actors in common with other such skilled artistes are specifically designated *kathputli nats*. The art of marionettery, practiced by these artistes, is claimed to have originated in the times of the celebrated king, Vikramaditya, whose throne with the 32 crowns possessed thirty-two puppets in motion (*simhasana battisi*). They were also honored by being called *raj-nats* (royal artistes) because they enjoyed immense prestige and were maintained by the king. They also produced a play on the king's life which remained popular for centuries.

The authentic period of Rajasthani puppetry commenced, however, with the reign of Amar Singh Rathore of Nagpur, who was a devoted patron of the arts and whose name is inseparably linked with the most well-known traditional puppet play of Rajasthan, *Amar Singh Rathore*. This play has become the stock-in-trade of all Rajasthani puppeteers, who have immmortalized the king's exploits in this fascinating manner. The other popular theme played is *Dhola Maru*.[3]

Unlike other forms of marionettes that often have many strings, a *kathputli* figure is manipulated with only one or two strings that are looped over the hands of the puppeteer. The ends of one string are attached to the head and back of the puppet; the ends of the other string

Double-faced *Kathputli* **figure approximately twenty-two inches high.** *Courtesy Margo Lovelace. (Photo by David L. Young)*

are attached to the hands of the figure. The heads of the one-and-a-half-foot-high puppets are carved from a single block of wood—most often mango. Their arms and hands are made from fabric that is stuffed with a springy, fibrous substance that allows for great flexibility of

Modern, legless *Sakhi-Nata* figure from Orissa. *Author's collection. (Photo by David L. Young)*

movement. The puppets have long skirts that reach to the ground. When cleverly manipulated, these skirts help to disguise the fact that the figures have no legs.

The *kathputli* cast of characters includes a number of stock types.

For example, there are dancing girls who, with the aid of straight pins placed at the tips of their hands, can be made to lift the hems of their dresses as they gracefully swirl and glide about the stage. There is the *kuchi* horse and rider puppet, whose elaborate tricks belie the simplicity of its operation. Fierce-looking warrior puppets, who carry a sword in one hand and a shield in the other are predictably popular. Other traditional characters are the juggler and the snake charmer and his snake.

The portable stage on which the *kathputlis* appear is a model of simplicity. A brightly colored front cloth and a black backdrop are suspended between two poles or, more often, between up-ended Indian bedframes known as *charpoys*. The major characters are suspended by their strings from a length of bamboo and lined up across the stage in front of the backdrop. This group is called the *durbar* or court. When a figure is ready to be used its strings are unwound from the bamboo and the puppet is moved forward.[4]

Although the *kathputli* puppeteers stand on the ground, the stage on which their puppets move is often raised some eighteen to twenty inches off the ground in order to provide the audience with a better view of the action. There is no scenery, as such, and no properties except for those which are integral parts of a puppet, such as the sword and shield of the warrior or the flute of the snake charmer. During evening performances, kerosene lamps, oil lamps, or electric lights are placed at either side of the stage in order to provide illumination. Photographs of *kathputli* theaters can be found in Bil Baird's *The Art of the Puppet*,[5] and in J. Tilakasiri's *The Puppet Theatre of Asia*.[6]

Puppet voices are provided by means of a bamboo and leather instrument that is held in the puppeteer's mouth and emits a high-pitched, reedy sound. Although the Rajasthani puppeteers do not literally speak for the puppets, all of the necessary moods and emotions are conveyed by a combination of expressive movement and the ingenious use of this tiny instrument.

A woman serves as interpreter at most performances even though the vocabulary of movement is usually quite clear to most members of the audience:

For example, conversation is shown by bringing the mouth of one puppet to the ears of another by jerking the strings of both the puppets. Anger is shown by a quick jerk of the puppet with a slight movement of the hand. Laughter is shown by jerking the puppet in such a way that the shoulders make quick upward and downward movements. Indifference or rather contempt and anger, is shown by turning one puppet away from another puppet, bringing the latter around to face the first puppet and repeating this several times.

Group of miniature puppets—approximately twelve inches high— manufactured in the style of *Bomallatam* figures from Madras. *Author's collection. (Photo by David L. Young)*

Fighting puppets are moved towards each other with great speed, and with swords and other weapons in their hands. . . . Greeting and saluting is done by bending the puppets and leaving their arms to hang loosely. Rebuking and beating is done by throwing one puppet on to the other. An affectionate greeting is shown by bringing the shoulders of two puppets together.[7]

The Rajasthani marionette company consists of at least three people: a singer-interpreter—usually a woman—a drummer, and, of course, a puppeteer. Each of them has a sophisticated awareness of what the puppets can and cannot do. They have learned the art of working together in order to make their puppets "speak" through music, sound, and expressive movement. Undoubtedly, many of the traditional and apparently simple bits of theatrical business have been polished and handed down through centuries of folk tradition.

Formerly, these traditions extended even to the discarding of puppets that were no longer useful. After a *kathputli* was worn and broken it was placed in a sacred river so that it could flow with the currents back to its celestial home.

The *kathputli* style has had strong influences on other types of Indian string puppetry, most notably those of the state of Orissa, which borders the Bay of Bengal on India's east coast. These string puppets are known as *sakhi-nata* or *kandhai-nata*.

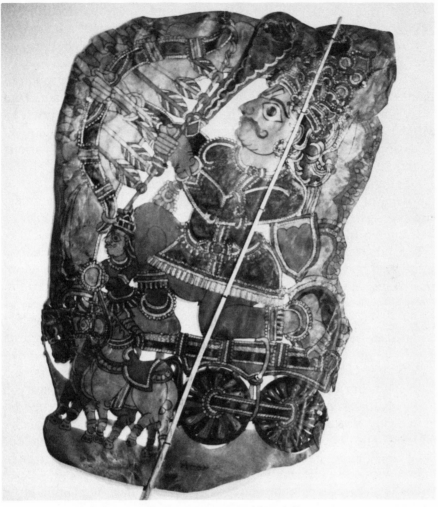

An elaborate but unarticulated *Togalu Bombe* **puppet from the state of Mysore. The height of the figure, excluding the control rod, is approximately twenty-five inches.** *Courtesy Alan G. Cook. (Photo by Alan G. Cook)*

The word *nata* means dance, *sakhi* means maidens, and *kandhai* means dolls. Orissan puppets are made from very light wood or papier-mâché. Each one is jointed and strung according to the action it will perform. The soldier doing tricks on horseback, the dancing girl, and the circus boy playing with a ball, all have to be made to suit the needs of their individual roles. The control is either a simple rod or a triangular wooden frame.

Orissa is home to two similar types of string puppets. In south Orissa, the figures have legs and are usually between nine inches and two feet high. Puppets of the more common type, which are popular throughout Orissa, do not have legs. A skirtlike garment known as a *ghagra* helps to disguise this fact. These figures vary in height between nine and eighteen inches.

After all of the pieces of a puppet have been carved to the required shapes, they are covered with a special base paint that is made from chalk powder mixed with gum. The resulting porous surface is covered with a priming coat that is buffed smooth. All of the surfaces that will be visible to the audience are then painted in detail with various brightly colored varnishes.

Most of the plots of the plays are drawn from traditional stories of the lives of the legendary heroes, Krishna and Rama. Sometimes, however, elements of the text are borrowed from the writings of well-known Indian poets.

The most common traditional stage is a simple cloth backdrop suspended between two poles. The puppeteer stands behind the cloth and manipulates his puppets in front of it. Depending on the circumstances, a bed turned on its side, a mat, or a simple sheet of cloth may serve as a stage. Since few of the Orissan traveling companies have much money to spare, decoration of the stage is usually minimal.

A typical Orissan puppet theater company has five members: the puppeteer, one helper, one drummer, and two narrators. The story is told in dialogue and traditional song. The spoken portions are rendered in a highly stylized fashion that conforms to the movement of the puppets. The puppeteer and his helper stand behind the backdrop, but the drummer and the narrator sit to one side of the front of the stage in full view of the audience.

The drummer signals the start of the performance by beating out a series of complicated rhythms. As the audience quiets down, one of the narrators sings an introductory song and the play begins. Although the substance of the play is usually quite serious, there are a great many short, farcical scenes, which have no relation to the plot. These provide comic relief—necessary changes of pace to help ensure the attention of the audience.

A form of string puppetry known as *bomalattam* is very popular in many parts of south India, particularly in Madras. The *bomalattam* has a long association with religious festivals and magic. In former times, performances were often commissioned in the belief that they would bring rain or prevent the spread of disease.

Most of the plays are based on Hindu legends; Tilakasiri has noted that the *Harischandra* and *Rukmangada* are favorite stories.[8] The *Harischandra* is the story of the noble and virtuous king, Harischandra. The *Rukmangada* details the complicated love story of Krishna and Rukmini and how the two of them triumph over Rukmini's evil brother, Rukma.

Bomalattam figures are two or three feet tall and are operated from above by a combination of rods and strings. The rods are attached to the puppet's hands, while the strings that control the puppet's head and body are attached to a wire or metal band that the puppeteer wears around his head. Performances are always accompanied by music and the puppeteers are justly famed for the skill with which they can make their figures appear to execute the complicated folk dances of the region, especially the *bharatya natyam*. The religious and moral themes of the plays are interspersed with lively humor and "tend to rouse religious humor to such an extent that they are considered even more effective than direct religious instruction."[9]

The *bomalattam* figures have wooden heads, arms, and hands and are beautifully dressed with jewelry, elaborate headdresses, and colorful costumes. A peculiar characteristic of this form is the carving of the hands, which are almost always made so that the thumb and index finger form a circle; the other three fingers are carved together in a straight line with the rest of the hand.

The portable stage for a *bomalattam* performance is about twenty feet long with a proscenium opening that is about ten feet wide and three feet high. It is backed by a decorated cloth screen that is approximately three and a half feet high. The whole stage house is about eight feet high and is covered with a thatched roof. In former times, lighting was accomplished by two oil lamps placed at either end of the stage. Today, successful companies usually have one or two electric stage lights that provide illumination.

Large style *bomalattam* puppets can still be found in the northeastern part of Madras. These puppets are often four feet high and weigh as much as one hundred pounds.

As in the puppet plays of Orissa, serious and farcical elements are alternated in the *bomalattam* performances in order to help ensure audience interest. Enthusiastic spectators sit or stand all night to watch performances that move them sometimes to laughter, sometimes to tears, and often to spontaneous bursts of applause.

The terms *gombeyata, sutrada-bombe*, and *yakshagana* all refer to a special form of string puppetry that was found in the state of Mysore on India's southwest coast.

Yakshagana puppets of the Karnatak coast were wooden string figures that were simply dressed but elaborately decorated with bits of colored glass as well as with the bodies and wings of green beetles. Music was of particular importance to this form and the chief

Bengali rod puppet or *Patul Nautch* figure. *Courtesy Alan G. Cook. (Photo by Alan G. Cook)*

puppeteer, called the *bhagavatar*, was responsible for the proper coordination of the puppet drama with its musical accompaniment.

Referring to this form, Tilakasiri says:

> The puppet play was so popular in the folk theatre of Karnatak that it became an integral part of every festival held there. In the coastal areas of the Karnatak country puppets are placed in temple cars and

Bengali rod puppet or *Patul Nautch* **figure.** *Courtesy Alan G. Cook. (Photo by Alan G. Cook)*

drawn in procession on festival occasions. The puppet show held the stage for years and attained great popularity in the Vijayanagar period (1336–1565). The Karnatak puppet show draws its themes from the Epics with titles such as *Vatsala Harana, Sri Krishan Sandhana, Krishnarjuna Yuddha, Subhadrakalyana* and *Ravanasamhara*. The learned brahmins of the south specialized in it and formed a separate class who used the word for "puppet"— *Gombe*—as a family name, viz., Gombe Anantachar.[10]

The *yakshagana* style, which had its origins in the ninth century A.D., "died a fiery death on 13th March 1928 in the great fire at the village of Issuru, where all the puppeteers had congregated at a fair. The terrible fire broke out at night destroying all of the puppets, save one . . . which is said to have been salvaged by an old artist."[11]

Bil Baird, in his book *The Art of the Puppet*, mentions string marionettes from Kerala called *pavakali*,[12] but says nothing about how they are used or the plays in which they appear.

In addition to its many types of string puppets, India is home to several styles of shadow puppetry. The sole surviving example of shadow puppetry in north India is the *Ravana chaya*, which is native to Orissa. Ravana, an important character in the great Hindu epic the *Ramayana*, is the ten-headed demon-King of Ceylon. The puppets, which are usually from nine inches to a foot high, are smaller than most other types of Indian shadow figures. They are cut from deerskin and are played against a white screen that is about six feet high and fourteen feet long. A performing company consists of one narrator who sits in front of the screen and two puppeteers. There are no musicians. The *Ravana chaya* is now rarely performed and was probably never a major form of Indian shadow theater.

The true home of the shadow puppet theater is south India. In fact, several scholars maintain that south India is the point of origin for shadow puppetry throughout the world.

A type of shadow theater with quasireligious significance known as *togalu bombe* is found in the south Indian state of Mysore. The articulated figures are elaborately incised from thin sections of carefully colored, translucent goatskin, deerskin, or buffalo hide. As in all forms of shadow theater, silhouettes of the figures are cast against a thin, white screen so that what the audience sees resembles a modern, animated film cartoon. The actors move the puppets, sing, and play musical instruments in order to help breathe life into their performances.

A prayer for rain is often accompanied by a performance of the *togalu bombe*, although shows are also staged for sheer entertainment. As with most other forms of Indian shadow puppetry, the plays are based on legends drawn from the *Ramayana* and the *Mahabharata*. An important part of a *togalu bombe* performance—which lasts from a half hour or so after sundown until dawn—is the bawdy, comic byplay between the ugly Killekyata and his shrewish wife, Bangarakka.

Black and white, beautifully incised, unarticulated leather shadow puppets called *pavaikoothu*, or the similarly styled and constructed *chakkla gombai atta*, are still used by itinerent puppet players along

India's southeastern coast. The puppets are usually made from goatskin and are about two and one half feet high. *Pavaikoothu* puppeteers can easily transport all of their equipment with them. Thirty or forty flat puppets, a screen, a portable lamp, and perhaps a harmonium are all they need to carry. These shows are noteworthy not so much for their delicacy of movement as for the urgency and excitement that is generated by the singers and musicians who accompany the performances.

The coastal areas of Mysore and Kerala are known as India's Malabar Coast. In the central portion of this region, there is an interesting form of shadow play called *nangyar koothu*. Performances are usually given in temples. A screen that is about eighteen yards long and about five feet high is set on a three- or four-foot-high wall:

> The screen is marked off into two divisions by a wooden pole that passes through the center to the roof of the *Koothu Madom* or playhouse. The right side is reserved for noble characters of the play like Rama, Sita, Hanuman and their allies. The left side is for the evil characters like Ravana and company. . . . All of the puppets are pinned to the screen with thorns. They are unpinned when required for manipulation.[13]

The performances are preceded by spectacular rituals and ceremonies that may take two hours or more. The basic elements of the performances are vigorous drum rhythms, the limited but affecting movements of the puppets, and, most importantly, the eerie wailing and chanting of the storyteller/puppeteers. More than most puppet theater forms in India, the *nangyar koothu* is dependent on the evocative and poetic power of the scripts. The basic language used is Tamil, although there is also a strong element of Malayalam.

Perhaps the most spectacular of the Indian shadow puppet forms is the *tholubomalatta*, which comes from Andhra Pradesh on India's southeastern coast. These articulated figures are made from either deer or buffalo hide and are often four or five feet high. The head and body of a *tholubomalatta* figure are supported by a split cane, and the movable arms are controlled by two or more canes that are attached to the wrists of the puppet. The articulated lower legs are not controlled and move freely back and forth as if to punctuate the actions of the figure. As in the Chinese shadow theater, the puppets often have interchangeable heads. The methods of manipulating *tholubomalatta* are remarkably similar to those of the *wayang kulit* puppets of Indonesia, which will be discussed later. In fact, some historians believe that the *tholubomalatta* are the direct ancestors of both the

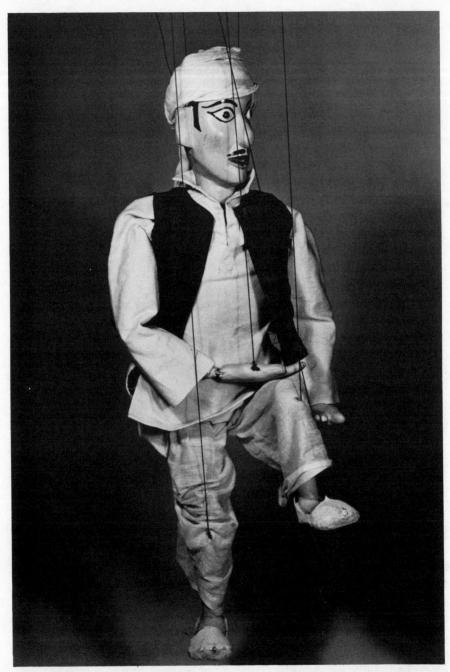

This puppet of a village leader from a contemporary Indian family planning play shows the influence of the Rajasthani *Kathputli* tradition. The arms, legs, and head of the twenty-eight-inch-high figure are carved from wood. The torso is a fabric bag stuffed with sawdust. *Author's collection. (Photo by David L. Young)*

This "villainess" from an Indian government-sponsored family planning play is about twenty-six inches high. *Author's collection. (Photo by David L. Young)*

Chinese shadow puppets and the Indonesian shadow theater.

The *tholubomalatta* screen is large—approximately seven feet high and twenty feet long. Manipulation of the figures is a difficult art. In addition to moving the figures themselves, the puppeteers dance and stamp on heavy wooden planks, in order to provide appropriate sound effects. Once again, the central stories are drawn from the *Mahabharata* and the *Ramayana*. Performed in temple grounds or village squares, these shows have, for centuries, been a part of village life in south India.

Although rod puppetry is relatively uncommon in India, West Bengal is home to a type of large rod puppet known as *patul nautch*. Carved from wood or made from a clay, rice, and hay mixture that is molded over an armature, the puppets are often four and a half feet high and are manipulated by a simple combination of strings and rods. The puppeteer tucks the central control rod into a belt at his waist and manipulates the puppet while dancing to the music of drums and cymbals.

India also has a large number of hand puppeteers who perform at fairs as well as on village and city streets. Several years ago, while working in India, I encountered a number of such itinerent showmen, each working in his own individual style with his own, usually contemporary subject matter.

Hand puppetry in Orissa, known as *gopa lila*, is famous for its representations of anecdotes from the life of Shri Krishna and his consort, Rada. These figures, which are made from cloth, wood, papier-mâché, and paint are usually from six inches to one foot high. The puppeteer has a partner who plays the drum and helps with the songs and dialogue. The two of them travel from house to house, using the box in which the puppets are carried as a stage.

The hand puppets of Kerala are made from clay, paper, and wood. They are decorated and costumed in imitation of the spectacular costumes and makeup of *kathakali* dancers. There is also some glove puppetry in the state of Madras that is loosely based on the hand puppet traditions of Kerala.

Although many of the traditional forms of puppetry are disappearing, the Indian goverment actively supports the art by hiring professional puppeteers to stage various kinds of educational shows throughout the country. Nonetheless, despite this practice and despite recent attempts by various cultural organizations to preserve the traditional art forms of India, it is likely that in another few decades, much of the folk puppetry of the nation will have disappeared forever.

Marionette clown, *Konangi*, from Ceylon. Probably dating from the first quarter of the twentieth century, it was recently recostumed. *Courtesy Alan G. Cook. (Photo by Alan G. Cook)*

SRI LANKA

Puppetry in Sri Lanka—or Ceylon, as it was formerly called—is closely related to the forms and styles of Indian puppet theater. One of the most popular styles of puppetry in Sri Lanka strongly resembles the Rajasthani *kathputli* tradition that was discussed earlier.

More importantly, Sri Lanka has an indigenous tradition of puppet theater that has evolved from the now almost extinct form of "live" folk drama known as *nadagama*. *Nadagama* was a comic folk opera style that became quite popular in the late nineteenth century. By the early years of this century, enterprising puppeteers, many of them originally trained as *nadagama* performers, routinely borrowed *nadagama* plots, characters, dialogue, and musical accompaniments for their own puppet shows. Eventually, the tradition-bound *nadagama* declined in popularity while the less expensive and more flexible puppet productions became highly successful.

Today, the *nadagama* style puppet theater is most closely identified with southern Sri Lanka around Ambalangoda. But troupes performing in a similar style can also be found in the region surrounding the central hill city of Kandy as well as around Jaffna in the northernmost part of the country.

The figures used are four-foot-high string marionettes. They are fashioned from the easily carved wood of the *kaduru* tree, which is native to southern Sri Lanka. The theater is made from a few easily assembled screens, curtains, and decorative panels. Major scenes are played in the center of the stage while less important episodes are performed on stage left or right. The puppeteers manipulate their figures from a raised platform or bridge and are hidden from the audience by a series of black screens.

There are several interesting photographs of *nadagama* puppets in Tilakasiri's *The Puppet Theatre of Asia*.[14] Tilakasiri, a native of Sri Lanka, describes the principal characters of the *nadagama* style puppet show in the following manner:

The stock characters presented with every play are the *Konangi* or *Bahabhutaya* (clown), *Vidane* (a sort of village official who acts as an announcer), *Sellapillai* (Tamil word meaning "boyplayer"), and the "dancing girl," all of which are traditional puppets. The *Konangi* appear first, in a pair, performing an introductory dance. The "dancing girl," unlike the *Konangi, Sellapillai* and *Vidane*, all of which are borrowed from the *nadagama*, is an item introduced in the theatrical style. The former looks highly artificial in appearance and presentation when compared with the latter indigenous characters. The traditional puppeteers, however, attach much importance to the item of the "dancing girl," introducing it as the *pièce de résistance* of the show, and making her perform all of the movements of an accomplished danseuse. The puppeteers pay special attention to details of costume in the presentation of figures depicting royalty. Sri Wickrama ja Singha and his chieftains always appear on the stage clad in bright and glittering royal attire but they are more static figures than moveable puppets.[15]

Each of the traditional *nadagama* puppet companies have eight to ten members. Of these, five or six are experts in the manipulation of the figures and speak or chant the lines while the remaining members of the company play musical instruments and/or sing in accordance with the demands of the performance. The musicians tend not to be a part of the company itself and have found that with their highly specialized knowledge of *nadagama* songs and music, it is more profitable to hire themselves out to various companies on a day-to-day basis.

As in so many parts of Asia, this traditional form of puppet theater is not likely to survive the twentieth century. Government-sponsored attempts at revitalizing this puppet form have met with only indifferent success, and newer generations of puppeteers are turning to hand and rod puppets and disregarding the complicated motifs of the *nadagama*.

NOTES

1. William Ridgeway, *The Dramas and Dramatic Dances of the Non-European Races* (Cambridge: Cambridge Press, 1915), p. 163.
2. Meher (Mrs.) Contractor, "Various Types of Traditional Puppets in India." *Marg—A Magazine for the Arts* (Bombay: Marg Publications, 1968), p. 5.
3. J. Tilakasiri, *The Puppet Theatre of Asia* (Ceylon: Dept. of Cultural Affairs, 1969), p. 18.
4. Bil Baird, *The Art of the Puppet* (New York: Macmillan, 1965), p. 46.
5. Ibid., p. 51.
6. Tilakasiri, *The Puppet Theatre of Asia*, pp. 119–21.
7. D. L. Samar, "Puppets and Puppeteers of Rajasthan," *Puppet Theatre Around the World*, ed. Som Benegal (New Delhi: Bharatya Natya Sangh, 1960), pp. 66–67.
8. Tilakasiri, *The Puppet Theatre of Asia*, p. 20
9. Ibid., pp. 20–21.
10. Ibid., p. 21.
11. Contractor, "Various Types of Traditional Puppets in India," p. 3.
12. Baird, *The Art of the Puppet*, p. 55.
13. K. B. Iyer, "Shadow Play in Malabar," *Marg—A Magazine for the Arts*, p. 24.
14. Tilakasiri, *The Puppet Theatre of Asia*, p. 122.
15. Ibid., p. 33.

5

A Pleasure Eternally New
The Puppets of China

The history of the Chinese puppet theater is steeped in mystery and uncertainty. One problem is that in the Mandarin Chinese language the same word, *kuei lei hsi,* is used for puppet performances as well as for performances with masks. As a result, it is often difficult for scholars such as Sun Kai-ti, the author of *The Origins of the Chinese Puppet Theatre* (written in Chinese and as yet untranslated into English), to tell whether certain important documents referred to puppets or to masked actors.

The earliest known Chinese legend that refers unmistakably to puppets concerns the puppet master Yan Shih, who performed in the court of the Chu emperor Mu Wang during the tenth century B.C. During the course of one particular performance, Mu Wang became convinced that the puppets were winking and behaving disrespectfully in the presence of his wives and courtiers. In a rage, the emperor ordered his executioner to slay the puppeteer immediately. But before the executioner could approach him, Yan Shih destroyed his puppets in order to show the emperor that they were only made of cloth and wood. Somewhat mollified, Mu Wang ordered the puppet show to continue—under the condition that women be forbidden to watch. This tradition of not allowing women to see puppet shows continued until the early years of the twentieth century.

Another ancient legend that dates from the third century B.C. describes the use of puppets in warfare. The leaders of the besieged

Hand puppet character from a Taiwanese television show has movable eyes and mouth as well as articulated hands. It represents a refined version of the traditional hand puppet styles. *Author's collection. (Photo by David L. Young)*

city of Pinchen ordered a puppet to be made in the likeness of an extraordinarily beautiful woman. When completed, it was displayed in various places along the walls of the city. The general of the opposing forces was so captivated with the face and figure of the "woman" that his wife, who was accompanying him, grew jealous and persuaded him to lift the siege and return home.

Sergei Obraztsov, in his important book, *The Chinese Puppet Theatre,* notes that:

This eight-inch-high professional hand puppet from mainland China is thought to be about seventy-five years old. Spots on cheeks and forehead are places where paint has flaked off. *Courtesy Margo Lovelace. (Photo by David L. Young)*

Neither of these legends of course reveal the origins of the puppet theatre in China, but their existence is evidence of the fact that, already in very early times, the puppet theater was part and parcel of the everyday social life of the people and clearly existed as a form of popular entertainment. The custom of forbidding women to witness puppet performances was in no way connected with the fact that the puppets winked at the Imperial wives, but the mention of this prohibition strengthens the probability of the existence of the puppet theatre in the epoch. The prohibition against women being present at such performances as spectators, arose from the widespread absence of women's rights in the feudal East and was typical not only of old China.[1]

At different periods, all major forms of puppetry—hand, shadow, string, and rod—reached an extremely high degree of development in China. Three other forms of puppetry—water puppets, powder or firework puppets, and live puppets—are also mentioned in the histories of the art but there is little information available on them. The following scanty information on these forms by Obraztsov is the most complete account in English.

"Powder puppets" no longer exist, nor is there any extant description of their construction. These puppets were probably set in motion by some mechanical device, where the dynamic force was provided in the form of a powder explosion, i.e., something like the contemporary combustion engine. We ought, therefore, to describe these as "pyrotechnic" puppets.

As for "floating puppets," the evidence is somewhat greater, but still too meagre for us to imagine what a performance was like. These were constructed in human form, but only from the waist upwards, and rested on cross-shaped or circular wooden bases, which enabled them to float on park lakes.

Sun Kai-ti writes that "live" puppet performances were characteristic of the Sung epoch only. These were, in fact, children in costume, sitting on the shoulders of grown-ups and imitating the movements of puppets.[2]

The oldest of the Chinese puppet theater forms is most likely hand puppetry. Performed either by a single puppeteer or by a troupe consisting of several artists, the form became well established in many parts of the country and today, on both Taiwan and the mainland, it is, perhaps, more popular than ever before.

Traditionally, there were seven men in a hand puppet theater troupe. Two of them were responsible for manipulating the puppets and speaking the roles. The remaining five were musicians who accompanied the performances and provided all of the necessary sound effects.

Individual puppeteers or groups of puppeteers carried their own portable theaters of varying designs. The hand puppet troupes presented their plays on a raised stage area that was usually about three feet high, four feet wide, and two feet deep. Despite the fact that they were often elaborately carved and decorated, such theaters were always relatively light and portable. Since China's hand puppet theater

Group of five Taiwanese hand puppets. *Courtesy Alan G. Cook. (Photo by Alan G. Cook)*

was and remains primarily a popular medium, this factor of portability was consistently maintained despite many other developments and variations. In China, as elsewhere, the puppet theater was forced to travel to its audiences rather than the other way around.

The plots of the plays were often adapted from the novels of the Tang, Sung, Yuan, Ming, and Ch'ing dynasties. Fairy tales and folk stories were also common sources. Naturally, all of the stories were subject to the imaginative whims and predilections of individual puppeteers.

Hand puppet shows were and still are known by several different names. On Taiwan, *pu-tai-hsi*, or "cloth bag play," is the most common term. They are also called *chang-chung-hsi*, which means "inside the palm puppets," and *hsiao-lung*, or "small cage puppets." This latter name is explained by the fact that the properties, costumes, and other equipment of the live, legitimate theater were formerly transported in large bamboo baskets called *ta-lung*, or "large cage." It seemed only natural that the tiny, puppet theater should be called "small cage" or *hsiao-lung*. In the province of Canton, the form is called *shou-t'e ching*, or "hand held Peking Opera," and in the province of Chekiang it is called *mu-t'ai*, or "wooden play."

This rather wide selection of names helps to indicate something of the regional variations in the types and styles of the puppets and the shows. In some areas, the performances are large-scale affairs with several puppeteers and scores of figures, while in others, one person, carrying the simplest sort of stage works with only two or three puppets.

No matter what the style, the care and discipline that the Chinese hand puppeteer devotes to his art are reflected in a common saying among the puppet masters of China: "There are 360 professions in the world but the hardest to master is the *pu-tai-hsi*."[3]

The first step toward the mastery of hand puppetry is "the training and art of the hands."[4] Aspiring puppeteers must learn to keep their arms raised for a half an hour without supporting or moving them. Then, they practice the intricate finger and hand movements that are necessary for the proper and expressive manipulation of the figures. Fledgling puppeteers are expected to understand the significance of the terms *straight, firm,* and *steady. Straight* refers to the puppet's body position. The puppeteers learn to use their forefingers to hold and control the puppets' heads so that the body and the head of the figures are always in the proper relationship. In this way, the puppet does not lean uncontrollably backward or foreward or to one side or the other. *Firm* is a term referring to the puppet's body expression. The puppeteer learns to hold the puppet so that there is no unintentional or unpurposeful movement. Because even a small gesture takes on magnified significance in the tiny hand puppet theater, emphasis is placed upon the exercise of great restraint in moving the puppets. *Steady* refers to the stage position of the puppet. The figure is held so that it does not bob up and down and so that it is held neither too high nor too low in relation to the stage and the audience.

The next step is learning to speak and sing in a distinctive voice for each of the basic characters in the *pu-tai-hsi*. These include: Kung-Mo, the white-bearded old man; Lau-Shêng, the old man; Hsiao Shêng, the young man; Hsiao-Tan, the young girl; Tao-Hua, the noble man; Wu-Shêng, a knight; Lao-Po, and old female clown; Lau-Tan, an old woman; and Hsiao-Hsi, a child.

These characters are expressed, in part, by the symbolic use of colors. For example, a white face blending into a rosy pink on the cheeks or brows signifies nobility and a strong sense of honor, while a face that is pure white reveals a duplicitous and deeply villainous nature. A red face indicates loyalty, honor, and courage. The black-faced character is even more loyal—often to the point of

97

This finely made Peking shadow figure is about nine inches high, excluding control rods. *Courtesy Ellen Proctor. (Photo by David L. Young)*

self-sacrifice. Individuals with crude or rough manners but courageous and honest souls have blue faces. Devils have green faces. A face with gold on it signifies that the character is purely or partly supernatural. Yellow-faced characters have well-disguised reserves of strength and cleverness.

The heads of Chinese hand puppets are usually rather small. Carved

Wayang kulit **leather shadow figure from Java.** *Courtesy Margo Lovelace.*
(Photo by David L. Young)

W.P.A. string puppets of a tomato and a carrot. *Courtesy Margo Lovelace. (Photo by David L. Young)*

Nang talung **shadow figure of flying prince from Thailand.** *Courtesy Alan Sugar. (Photo by David L. Young)*

Wooden Taiwanese hand puppet from a popular television show made in the traditional manner. *Author's collection. (Photo by David L. Young)*

Early twentieth-century Sicilian rod puppets. *Courtesy Margo Lovelace. (Photo by David L. Young)*

This toy marionette from the Chinese mainland made in the traditional manner dates from the early 1960s. *Courtesy Alan G. Cook. (Photo by Alan G. Cook)*

from wood or carefully made from papier-mâché that has been delicately shaped, painted, and laquered, they are rarely more than two and a half or three inches high. The hands and the feet are normally wooden and the bodies and headdresses are made from intricately embroidered silk or cotton cloth.

Hand puppetry, both in Nationalist China and the People's Democratic Republic, is still an active and developing art form.

The history of the famed Chinese shadow puppet theater, like that of the hand puppet theater, is intermingled with a number of early legends.

The most popular of these stories dates from the Han dynasty (206 B.C.–A.D. 220) and concerns the Emperor Wu Ti. The Emperor grew depressed after the death of his favorite mistress and began to neglect important state matters. Several members of his court grew concerned and offered a reward to anyone who could reunite the Emperor with his lady. Their problem was solved by a clever magician who made a translucent image of the girl and showed it against a lighted screen within the Imperial quarters. The figure was so like the girl and was made to move and speak so beautifully and convincingly that the Emperor's depression was cured and he quickly returned to the management of state business.[5]

Sun-kai-ti, the Chinese puppet theater historian who was mentioned earlier, believes that the shadow theater originated during the Tang epoch, sometime between the seventh and ninth century A.D., and was firmly established by the time of the eleventh century.[6] Until 1949, when the art was revived by the government of The People's Republic of China, shadow puppetry was primarily a form of amusement for the aristocratic and rich.

Unlike the hand puppet theater performances, from which women were excluded, the shadow plays were presented for audiences composed mainly of women, children, and servants. During the Ch'ing Dynasty (1644–1900), women of the upper classes were obliged to avoid the tea houses, the restaurants, the theaters, and the places of business and government that were the centers of the male dominated society under the emperors. Nonetheless, these women had a curiosity and intelligence that extended out into a world that was largely closed or forbidden to them. Unable to travel freely, rich and influential women found ways to bring the world to their own doorsteps.

In this world behind the vermilion doors the shadow players brought the drama of the outside universe. With some three hundred plays at its command, the entire repertory with actors, costumes, scenery, properties, orchestra and theatre itself could be transported on a small cart, and four men were enough to present the most elaborate spectacle. These men were usually provincials from the city of Lanchow which is the traditional home of the shadow drama. They were simple, hardworking craftsmen not tainted by the evil reputation that enshrouded the actors of the regular stage. . . . The audiences included not only the mistresses of the house, but the servants also; the interests were numerous and the ages diverse.[7]

Chinese shadow plays are concerned with military, civil, or religious themes and stories. The civil plays have always concentrated on the tragic or comic events in the everyday lives of ordinary people. Military plays are strongly based on historical events and have always focused on the intrigues and battles among the nobility of Imperial China. The religious plays are drawn from Confucian, Taoist, and Buddhist stories.[8]

Today, there are at least three distinct styles of Chinese shadows.

Antique Chinese marionette. *Courtesy Josie Robbins. (Photo by Alan G. Cook)*

Antique Chinese marionette. *Courtesy Josie Robbins. (Photo by Alan G. Cook)*

One style is found in the province of Szechuan. These figures are about thirty-six inches high and are made from buffalo leather. A second and more common type is popular in the vicinity of Peking—a city that has been at the hub of Chinese government and culture for hundreds of years. These figures are smaller, more delicately carved, and more beautifully colored than the shadows of Szechuan. They are usually about twelve inches high and are fashioned from a very thin leather made from the bellies of donkeys. A third form is popular on Taiwan. The figures are slightly larger and are more crudely made than those from Peking.

In all these styles, the deceptively simple method of articulation, in the hands of expert operators, can produce a range of movement that is both wide and subtle. The figures are jointed at the shoulders, elbows, wrists, hips, and knees. Three control wires are connected to each figure, one to the neck and one at each wrist. The lower ends of these wires are inserted into bamboo dowels in order to facilitate handling. The bodies are made with a special collar that permits the heads to be easily removed and interchanged. In this way, a single character can be made to change expression; or a large number of characters who would

Antique Chinese marionette. *Courtesy Josie Robbins. (Photo by Alan G. Cook)*

logically be dressed similarly and do not have to appear on stage at the same time, can be presented without the necessity of creating a separate body for each. The scenery, although usually quite elaborate, is cut from leather and constructed so that it can be easily packed for travel.

The puppeteers are responsible for manipulating the puppets and speaking the lines. Often, performances are accompanied by a small orchestra.

Although many of the contemporary figures are still made of leather, the use of a translucent plastic is becoming more and more common. Many connoisseurs feel that this trend signals a deterioration in the traditional form. Others are persuaded that the change in materials represents a perfectly natural step in the evolution of an ancient yet modern art form—a form that still flourishes in the provinces of Chekiang, Kuangtung, Hunan, Hopei, Shuntung, Shesi, and Heilungtang.

The Chinese tradition of string puppetry is also impressive. When the Soviet master puppeteer Sergei Obraztsov visited the People's Republic of China in the late 1950s, he was clearly amazed:

Rod puppets of the Chinese mainland dating from before 1930. *Courtesy Alan G. Cook. (Photo by Alan G. Cook)*

As far as Chinese puppets are concerned, the control of movement has been worked out and elaborated by a tradition to a degree which I could never possibly have imagined. I have seen puppets operated by twenty, thirty and even forty strings and I have seen them move their mouths, their eyes and their eyebrows. I have seen astonishingly expressive mimicry on puppet faces resulting from the movements of brow and chin, and finally I have seen literally living hands capable of grasping any object.[9]

The complicated techniques of Chinese marionette construction and manipulation have probably evolved over the course of two or three thousand years. Bil Baird's *The Art of the Puppet* shows an interesting painting from the Ming Dynasty (1368–1644)—the original of which is in the British Museum.[10] It shows a group of puppeteers playing on a raised platform accompanied by a pair of musicians who stand offstage to the left of the performers. The puppeteers in the picture use a type of paddle-shaped control that is still common in China. Their puppets do not look particularly complicated and seem to have only six or seven strings. Despite the fact that throughout most of their history, Chinese string puppeteers were, at best, only semiliterate, they eventually produced what are probably the world's most technically sophisticated types of string puppets.

There are famous string puppet theaters in Chekiang, Shensi,

Antique Chinese rod puppet heads. Figure on right had movable eyes, one of which is now lost. Head on left was not articulated. *Private collection. (Photo by Alan G. Cook)*

Kuantung, and Western Fukien—each of which has developed its own individual style. According to Obraztsov's account dating from the late fifties, string puppetry was extremely popular. He says: "In the whole of China, there are more than one thousand puppet and shadow theatres."[11] He points out that in 1954, ". . . in one district alone—Shanhan in Western Fukien—there were fifty troupes of actors using string puppets."[12] There is no reason to believe that these impressive numbers have diminished. In fact, it seems more likely that on both the mainland and on Taiwan, string puppetry is now more popular than ever before.

A form that has been growing in popularity in China as well as the rest of the world is the rod puppet. As with the other types of figures, the Chinese operate their rod puppets with consummate skill. The high level of technical facility is, again, the product of centuries of gradual development.

Marjorie Batchelder has indicated that the traditional rod puppet theaters were divided into two broad types. The first, called *t'o ho kung hsi*,[13] was highly literate and was performed for rich or aristocratic audiences. She describes the second type in the following manner:

The plays given by the poor itinerant puppeteers are called *Ho Ern Li Tzu* and are similar to the *T'o Ho Kung Hsi* only in the way they are performed, because they have no literary origin, the singing is unpolished and the acting inadequate. The puppets and costumes are much less complex.[14]

Today, throughout Taiwan and the mainland, rod puppetry is as popular as it ever was. In fact, all of the traditional puppet forms are being carefully nurtured and developed, particularly in The People's Democratic Republic. As a fortunate result, it looks as though China's traditional and folk forms of puppet theater will be around for some time to come.

NOTES

1. Sergei Obraztsov, *The Chinese Puppet Theatre*. Trans. J. T. MacDermott. (London: Faber and Faber, 1961), p. 27.
2. Ibid., pp. 27–28.
3. Anon., "Chinese Puppet History." Unpublished material. (Taipei: Kuangchu Program Service, 1974), p. 1.
4. Ibid.
5. Benjamin March, *Chinese Shadow Figure Plays and Their Making* (Detroit: Puppetry Imprints, 1938), p. 12.
6. Obraztsov, *The Chinese Puppet Theatre*, p. 28.
7. March, *Chinese Shadow Figure Plays and Their Making*, p. 13.
8. John Bernard Myers, "Puppets Probably Preceded People on World's Stages," *Smithsonian* vol. 6, no. 2 (May 1975).
9. Obraztsov, *The Chinese Puppet Theatre*, p. 24.
10. Bil Baird, *The Art of the Puppet* (New York: Macmillan, 1965), p. 133.
11. Obraztsov, *The Chinese Puppet Theatre*, p. 33.
12. Ibid.
13. Marjorie Batchelder, *Rod Puppets of the Human Theatre* (Columbus: Ohio Univ. Press, 1947), p. 91.
14. Ibid., p. 42.

6

A People's Proud Heritage
The Wayang of Indonesia

Over the course of the last ten centuries, Indonesia has developed extraordinarily elaborate traditions of folk puppetry. Most of the important puppet theater activity has taken place on the island of Java, on the western end of which sits the Indonesian capital city, Djakarta. Equally elaborate traditions exist on the Indonesian island of Bali. In no other area of the world is puppetry so obviously linked to all of the arts of a region as it is in Indonesia. The terms, styles, themes, and motifs of Indonesian puppetry appear and reappear in Indonesian sculpture, painting, drama, music, and dance. In fact, it is virtually impossible to appreciate fully any of the traditional arts of Indonesia without a prior awareness of the stories, music, movement, and visual styles of the island's three major forms of folk puppetry: *wayang kulit*, *wayang klitik*, and *wayang golek*.

According to Claire Holt, the earliest Javanese use of the term *wayang* dates from A.D. 907.[1] Because *wayang* is a generic term for Javanese dance and theater, as well as puppetry, there is some disagreement among scholars concerning the derivation of this term.[2] Even so, there is general accord about its connection with shadows or silhouettes. Some experts believe that the word *wayang* refers to an ancient concept according to which all art is regarded as a shadow of life. Others interpret the term somewhat more literally and believe that it is the oldest term for *wayang kulit*, probably the most ancient of Java's puppet theater forms.

Wayang kulit encompasses three subtypes of shadow puppetry that differ principally in their story material: the *wayang gedog* deals with the Panji cycle, which is based on legends involving tenth-century

107

A Javanese *wayang kulit* **figure.** *Courtesy Margo Lovelace. (Photo by David L. Young)*

Javanese heroes; the *wayang madya* repertoire is based on the works of the nineteenth-century Javanese poet Ranggawarsita, while the *wayang purwa* concentrates on tales drawn from the great Hindu Indian epics, the *Ramayana* and the *Mahabharata*.

Because of its heaviest reliance on these traditional Hindu stories and legends, many experts believe that Indonesian shadow puppetry had its origins in the shadow puppet theater of India. Some time between the eleventh and fourteenth centuries, translated versions of the *Ramayana* and the *Mahabharata* were written down in old Javanese prose. In the process, the stories, although retaining most of the original Indian characters and episodes, acquired a distinctly Javanese style.[3]

The clown, *Gaveng*, a Javanese wayang kulit figure. *Courtesy Margo Lovelace.*
(Photo by David L. Young)

The period of Hindu cultural and political domination on Java lasted
from the second century A.D. until the middle of the fifteenth century,
when the Hindu Majapahit Empire was overthrown by the Moslems.
In order to preserve their ascendancy, the Moslems undertook a
deliberate policy of destroying or undermining what they could of the
still prevailing Hindu culture. Although the Moslems did manage to
destroy a great many individual works of art, it was impossible for
them to eradicate over a thousand years of Hindu influence. As a
result, a certain degree of cultural intermingling was unavoidable. It is
this aspect of the region's political and religious history that accounts
for the peculiar mixture of Hindu, Moslem, and native Javanese
elements inherent in all of the *wayang* forms.

109

Wayang kulit figures are highly stylized leather shadow puppets with long, graceful arms that are jointed at the shoulders and elbows. Each figure is controlled and supported by three thin rods made from carefully prepared buffalo horn. The most highly prized figures are made from very thin, translucent, buffalo calf skin.

The untreated skin is first rubbed with chalk or soot in order to remove the excess oils. It is then successively sun dried, smoothed out, soaked in water for several days, stretched on a special frame, and redried. After it is dry, the leather is finished by a laborious process that entails scraping, rubbing, and polishing. Next, the leather is cut into pieces. On each piece the outline of a puppet character is etched with a special needle. The figure is then painstakingly cut out, painted, and gilded in accordance with a complicated system of conventions and traditions.

The three control rods are cut, sized, and shaped according to necessity. The largest of these buffalo horn rods supports the body. The two smaller ones are used to control the arms. All three are attached to the leather figure with brass or silver thread or coconut fiber.

The identities and personality traits of the puppet figures can be determined, in part, by how they conform to the Javanese visual ideals of *alus*, or refinement, and *kazar*, or crudeness. The most refined characters have long, narrow eyes, thin lips, gracefully sloping foreheads, pointed noses, and lithe, graceful bodies. The legs are close together and the head is tilted slightly forward and downward—a traditional method of representing virtue, nobility, and intelligence. The cruder figures can be identified by their large, bulbous noses, rounded, bulging eyes, thick lips, and pointed teeth. *Kazar* characters tend to have large bodies with the feet planted widely apart as though they were constantly preparing to engage in battle. The puppets vary in height from about twelve inches to over three feet. Women and refined characters are usually the smallest figures; giants and *kazar* figures the largest.

According to Claire Holt, the facial coloring of a *wayang* puppet figure can be yet another clue to its identity, or at least to the emotional makeup of the character that the figure represents.[4] The most common colors are red, white, and gold. Blue and white are also used but much less frequently. Black symbolizes virtue, wisdom, and inner tranquility. Characters with red faces are rash, aggressive, and highly emotional. Gold usually denotes beauty, although Holt says that it may also be used by the puppet maker to enhance the beauty and value of the puppet, without regard to any kind of symbolism or dramatic significance. White usually denotes youth and beauty and blue seems

A Balinese *wayang kulit* **figure.** *Courtesy Alan G. Cook. (Photo by Alan G. Cook)*

to indicate cowardice. Because the *wayang* plays often deal with considerable spans of time, a single character may be represented by several different puppets, each with a different facial coloring. This is an important method of showing various stages in a character's development.

Other details such as the color and style of costume and the type of headdress can also help members of the audience to identify specific characters.

An Indonesian tapestry showing the events of a *wayang* performance in the manner of a *wayang beber* scroll. *Courtesy Margo Lovelace. (Photo by David L. Young)*

Javanese *wayang golek* **horse and rider.** *Courtesy Alan G. Cook. (Photo by Alan G. Cook)*

Generally speaking, noble or refined puppet figures in a *wayang kulit* performance can appear only on the right side of the shadow screen—from the *dalang's*, or puppeteer's, point of view; cruder characters can appear only on the left side. At the beginning, at the end, and at several times during the play, a special fan-shaped puppet called the *gunungan* appears on the screen. It represents a symbolic mountain or tree and depending upon how it is moved, it can represent any of a variety of obstacles, conflicts, and situations that the virtuous characters must overcome. Although unarticulated, the *gunungan* is always elaborately incised and painted. Before each performance, the *dalang* arranges the good and evil characters to his left and right against the screen by thrusting the sharply pointed rods into a soft, pulpy banana tree log that always lies at the base of the screen. The smallest figures are positioned closest to him and the larger figures are placed farthest away. The removal of the *gunungan* signals the start of the performance.

A *wayang kulit* performance normally lasts from an hour or so after sundown until dawn. In former times, the men in the audience sat on the same side of the shadow screen as the *dalang*, and could see the elaborate painting on the figures as well as the other elements of backstage activity while the women sat on the opposite side of the screen and viewed the figures in silhouette. According to legend, all audience members are protected from evil forces while a performance is in progress.

During a *wayang kulit* performance, the *dalang* sits behind the large, linen shadow screen, which is about twelve feet long and five feet high and stretched between two bamboo uprights. Beneath this screen is the banana log into which the puppeteer can easily stick the rods that help to support the puppets before and during a performance. Over the *dalang*'s head is a traditional copper lamp, called the *blentjong*, which is positioned so as to throw the puppets' silhouettes onto the screen. To his left is a wooden carrying chest for the puppets. During the performance, this box doubles as a simple percussion instrument. The *dalang* holds a small, wooden mallet between his toes and strikes the chest and/or some metal plates attached to it in order to provide sound effects and to signal the small orchestra known as the *gamelan*.

The *gamelan* plays a vital part in setting the moods and reinforcing the actions of the complex dramas. Its members sit behind the *dalang* and provide constant musical accompaniment at all performances. The basic instruments are drums, gongs, bells, flutes, xylophones, and a simple, two-stringed, violinlike instrument.

Dalangs have always been highly respected members of the Javanese artistic community. Their profession, which has its origins in sacred ritual, is considered to be both difficult and important. A *dalang*'s knowledge and skills can be divided into eight categories: (1) a knowledge of the appropriate history and legends; (2) an understanding of the many types of music that are such an important part of a *wayang* performance; (3) a complete familiarity with the spoken and chanted parts of the plays; (4) the ability to give total concentration to all aspects of performance; (5) the ability to speak all of the required dialects and modes of speech; (6) the ability to improvise various dramatic situations with both art and eloquence; (7) mastery of the spiritual essence of the stories, which includes both understanding them and the ability to communicate that understanding; and (8) the ability to manipulate the puppets and to handle the other physical and technical skills of performance.

The *wayang kulit* is popular among all classes and *dalangs* perform everywhere, from village squares to the homes of the rich and powerful. In the hands of a skilled *dalang* and an accomplished *gamelan* orchestra, a *wayang kulit* performance is both exquisitely beautiful and dramatically exciting. In former times, members of the nobility usually owned their own sets of *wayang kulit* figures. From time to time they would commission well-known *dalangs* to perform

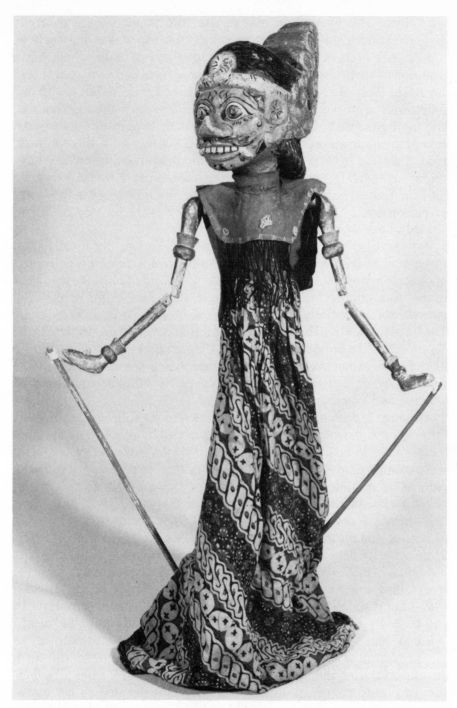

This fierce, Javanese *wayang golek* character is about twenty-inches high. *Author's collection. (Photo by David L. Young)*

with them. But even when not in use, the puppets were carefully displayed and highly regarded as works of art in and of themselves.

Just east of Java lies the Indonesian island of Bali, which has a tradition of shadow puppetry that is derived from and similar to that of Java. The Balinese tradition began some time between the twelfth and fourteenth centuries. Balinese *wayang kulit* are usually less stylized and more mechanically complicated that their Javanese counterparts. Javanese shadows are manipulated solely by means of three control rods. Balinese figures, while retaining the three rods, often also have more sophisticated string and spring mechanisms to help operate moveable jaws, arms, and legs.[5] There is also a difference in the styles of performance. Balinese shows rely much more heavily on broad comedy than those in Java.

Bali is also the home of a less well-known form of large, three-dimensional puppetry known as *barong landong*. From a photograph in Miguel Covarrubias's book, *Island of Bali*, these appear to be rod puppets that are approximately twice life size.[6] The puppeteers are entirely hidden under the long skirts of their puppets. The heads, arms, and bodies of the figures are carried on the heads and shoulders of the puppeteers. Despite the fact that the *barong landong* have holy significance and perform their dance-dramas inside temple walls, they delight their audiences primarily because of their wild dancing and comic bawdiness.

Although it does not seem to have much to do with puppet theater, the Javanese *wayang beber* is often mentioned by scholars as a puppet theater form. The characters and events of the *wayang beber* stories were painted onto long paper rolls that the *dalang* revealed, picture by picture, as he told the story. Some experts believe that the *wayang beber* is the oldest form of Indonesian puppetry. They base their opinion on its mechanical simplicity. But there seems to be no reason to assume that the mechanical simplicity of *wayang beber* has anything to do with its date of origin, and definite information concerning its history is very sparse. More than likely, it is simply a form of storytelling that shares the legends and visual style of the *wayang kulit*—but is not really a part of the tradition of Javanese puppetry. In any case, by all accounts it was never a particularly popular form.

Much more significant was the *wayang klitik*—also known as *wayang kelitik* or *wayang keruchil*. It has been suggested that this form developed during the fifteenth century as a medium for the presentation of purely historical stories—subjects not deemed to be appropriate material for the *wayang kulit*. Although *wayang klitik* performances are now rare, many of the puppets are in public and private collections throughout the world.

The visual style of *wayang klitik* puppets is very similar to that of the *wayang kulit* figures. However, unlike the flat, leather shadow puppets, the heads and bodies of the *wayang klitik* characters are carved in low relief on thin pieces of wood. The arms are usually made of leather and the whole figure is manipulated in much the same fashion as a *wayang kulit* puppet—with one control rod extending up through the body and one rod attached to each hand. *Wayang klitik* puppets are as carefully and elaborately painted as *wayang kulit* figures. The strong Middle Eastern elements in costume and decoration can be explained by the fact that the initial popularity of the form coincides with the earliest period of Moslem domination in Java.

It is common practice for scholars to trace a historical development from the totally flat *wayang kulit* puppets, through the more three-dimensional *wayang klitik* figures to the totally three-dimensional *wayang golek* rod puppets. While it is probably true that shadow puppets are the earliest form, the origins of the other two forms cannot be dated with any certainty. The apparent progression from flat figures to three-dimensional puppets is interesting but cannot be regarded as conclusive evidence that one form preceded another.

Some authorities, reflecting that the development of the *wayang golek* coincides with a period of Chinese settlement on Java, believe that this rod puppet style is a product of Chinese influence on older Javanese puppet traditions. On the other hand, American puppeteer Bil Baird has suggested that the form could have come from Bengal on the east coast of the Indian subcontinent.[7]

Whatever its origin, there is no doubt that the *wayang golek* became and remains a popular form of puppet theater in Java. As with all types of folk art, there is considerable variation in the artistic quality of *wayang golek* figures. In addition, because *wayang golek* is not subject to the same rigorous conventions as the *wayang kulit*, it is often virtually impossible to ascertain which character a particular figure is supposed to represent.

Wayang golek puppets are normally between fifteen and twenty inches high. The upper portion of the body is of carved wood that has a hole drilled through it from the top of the neck to the base of the torso. A hand-carved wooden control rod called a *gapit* fits through this hole so that an inch or two of its upper tip extends out through the top of the neck. Several inches of the *gapit* also extend down below the body in order to provide a firm hand-hold. The *gapit* widens below the torso section in order to keep the body of the puppet from slipping down onto the *dalang's* hand. The head of the figure is forced without glue or other fasteners onto the top of the *gapit*. By turning the *gapit* the puppeteer can turn the puppet's head independently of its body. All

These delicate Javanese *wayang golek* **women are each about fourteen inches high.** *Author's collection. (Photo by David L. Young)*

wayang golek figures have long batik skirts that serve to conceal the *dalang's* hand and forearm. Each puppet has delicately carved wooden arms that are jointed with string at the shoulders and elbows. These are controlled by two thin, wooden rods that are attached to the hands or wrists of the puppets. Despite such an apparently simple method of operation, an expert *dalang* can endow his figures with a range of expressive movement that is both wide and subtle.

Because it is considered a sacred art, great care is taken with all aspects of puppet performance on Java and Bali. Indonesian audiences still enjoy and venerate their puppet theater forms. In Indonesia—as elsewhere—increasing Western influence during the past few decades has had some unpleasant side effects. Untrained *"dalangs"* enjoy enthusiastic receptions from well-intentioned but undiscriminating tourist audiences, and the puppets are often cheaply made and mass produced for large-scale commercial sale as souvenirs. Fortunately, the taste for fine puppet theater is so deeply ingrained in Indonesian culture that excellent performances will undoubtedly be available for a long time to come—although probably in ever-decreasing quantity.

NOTES

1. Claire Holt, *Art in Indonesia* (Ithaca: Cornell Univ. Press, 1967), p. 128.
2. A. R. Philpott, *Dictionary of Puppetry* (Boston: Plays, Inc., 1969), pp. 227–28.
3. Marjorie Batchelder, *Rod Puppets and the Human Theatre* (Columbus: Ohio University Press, 1947), p. 4.
4. Holt, *Art in Indonesia*, pp. 142–43.
5. Batchelder, *Rod Puppets and the Human Theatre*, p. 18.
6. Miguel Covarrubais, *Island of Bali* (New York: Knopf, 1947), p. unnumbered.
7. Bil Baird, *The Art of the Puppet* (New York: Macmillan, 1965), p. 56.

7

Southeast Asia
The Crossroads of Puppetry

THAILAND

Thailand has sophisticated traditions of both shadow and rod puppetry. Both forms rely heavily on stories from the *Ramakien*, the Thai *Ramayana*, tales from Thai history and mythology, and plots drawn from the Indonesian tales of Panji. The earliest reference to Thai shadow puppetry occurred in 1458 in a law of King Boromatrailokanath. Rod puppetry achieved its greatest popularity during the last half of the nineteenth century. While the *nang*, or shadow performance, was usually a form of folk theater, *hun*, or rod puppet, performances were a traditional entertainment of the Thai aristocracy. Because the forms have existed more or less independently of one another, it is appropriate to discuss them separately.

There are really two types of Thai shadow puppets: the large *nang yai* and the much smaller, more popular, *nang talung*. The *nang yai* are huge, completely unarticulated shadow figures. According to J. Tilakasiri, writing in 1968, "The *nang yai*, the larger or bigger shadow figure, is no longer played."[1] However, an article in *Orientations*, "Giant Shadow Play of Thailand," by Euayporn Kerdchouay and Michael Smithies, makes it clear that at least one troupe of *nang yai* puppeteers was still performing as late as 1973. This troupe used three hundred and twenty figures that were made by three village craftsmen in 1862.[2]

The origins of the *nang yai* are obscure. Since their plays are drawn primarily from the legends of the *Ramayana*, it is often assumed that the form was adapted from the large shadow puppets of South India.

Kerdchouay and Smithies point out that: "Although the *Ramayana* and Buddhism are unconnected, they spread into the region from India at about the same time, and their development has been continuous but separate. The *Ramayana* was performed in India as a play and in Southeast Asia the story underwent changes in different countries; versions of the story written by local authors include national history and regional history."[3]

Crafting of the *nang yai* figures was a time-consuming and tedious process, but the results amply justified the methods. The leather was prepared from cow or buffalo hide that was soaked in a chalk or brine solution and then stretched over a bamboo frame and dried in the sun. Then it was scraped and rubbed in order to remove the hairs and sinews as well as to make it thinner. The prepared skin was then rubbed with a charcoal paste. An outline of the final design was drawn on the surface of the blackened leather in some light color. This drawing was carefully cut out with special tools in order to produce a complete leather figure that was then mounted on one or two slender, split bamboo rods.

The carefully incised *nang yai* puppets are often seven feet high and four feet wide. Some of the figures are dyed and some are not. According to Tilakasiri, the colored shadows were used for daytime performances and the uncolored figures were used at night.[4] In addition:

> If some parts of the figure are to remain a natural light brown color, a knife is used to scratch off the black charcoal coating; against the light and with the white screen behind, this brown part appears much lighter than the rest of the figure. Some figures are transparent and these, called crystal shadows (*nang keo*), are made from the skins of young buffalos or cows. If any part of the figure is to appear absolutely white, like for example, Sita's face, the leather has to be cut away. Often the whole female body is shown as white, and these figures are collectively known as outline figures (*nang naa kwat*). For an effect less pallid than this, more holes are made in the appropriate part of the figure so that more light can pass through. These holes give the texture of the picture; a tiled roof can be distinguished from an *atap* palm roof by the patterning of the holes on the leather. Different hole shapes are used for the different effects needed to represent the sky, rain, the earth, running water and so on.[5]

Some *nang yai* figures survive in private collections and Thai country temples. The Ledersmuseum in Offenbach, Germany, has a particularly fine set of figures.

Each puppet is operated by a single puppeteer. Holding their figures

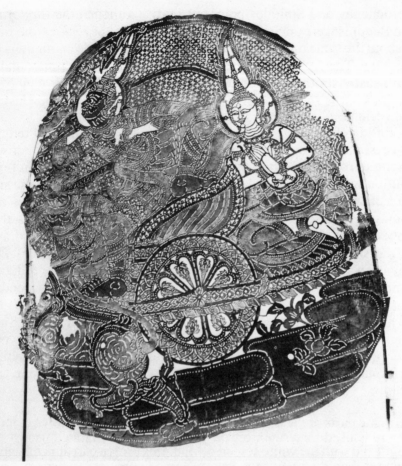

A giant Thai shadow puppet or *nang yai.* **Note that it depicts an entire scene rather than a single character.** *Courtesy Alan G. Cook. (Photo by Alan G. Cook)*

above their heads, the puppeteers dance the appropriate actions of the dramas while the story is sung or chanted by the narrators.

Most of the *nang yai* performances took place in front of the *jor nang*, or screen. However, when the troupe wished to suggest a great distance, the performers moved behind the screen and the action was seen by the audience as if through a haze. Usually, however, the area behind the screen was used only as a dressing room for the performers. Although there was no standard size for the *jor nang*, it had to be large enough to provide a backdrop for several figures and their operators to perform at the same time. Apparently, the screen was usually about forty feet long and about fourteen feet high.

There were usually about twenty people in a *nang yai* troupe: two narrators, six to ten actors/dancers/puppeteers, a sound effects person, a fire-tender, and an individual who arranged the figures offstage so that they could be picked up in the order required for a smooth and orderly performance.[6] Presumably, the remaining people served as musicians and/or provided other kinds of technical assistance.

Several scholars have noted the resemblances between the graceful movements of the *nang yai* puppeteers and those of the *Khon*, or Siamese classical dance. For example, Tilakasiri says:

It is . . . accepted on reliable evidence that the shadow play preceded the masked play and that the *nang* developed into the *Khon*. A transitional stage in this development was the use of the variety of dance called "Khon before the screen" where the actors danced in front of a screen of white cloth, similar to that used for the shadow play. The most striking evidence of the connection between the *nang* and the *Khon* is afforded by the use of side-long movements by masked players who are thus supposed to have imitated the hide figures which showed their profiles to the audience in the *nang*. Even the text-book of the masked plays is known to be identical with that of the shadow play used before the *Ramakien* was adopted for the latter.[7]

More popular and more enduring than the large *nang yai* figures are the much smaller *nang talung* figures, which are quite similar in form and style to the *wayang kulit* of Java. The characters and stories of both the Thai and Javanese puppets are quite similar, they are manipulated in much the same fashion, and they are accompanied by very similar style orchestras. *Nang talung* puppets usually have only one articulated arm. They are about fifteen inches high, brightly colored, and are normally made with the character in profile.

A single *nang talung* or *nang yai* puppet may represent two or more characters, plus a scenic background. In other words, one Thai shadow figure is often carved and painted to show a whole scene.

Although both the *nang talung* and the *nang yai* are probably of Indian ancestry, the arts, as they have ultimately emerged, are uniquely Thai.

Thai rod puppets are even more unusual. The most important information in English about these figures was written by Monti Tramote and appeared as the chapter "Thai Puppet Shows" in *Puppet Theatre Around the World*, edited by Som Benegal.

Thai rod puppets *(hun)* were larger and much more elaborately carved and costumed than the more well-known Javanese *wayang golek* figures. The most striking and elegant of the Thai rod puppets were about three feet high and were manipulated by a complicated system of internal strings as well as by rods. Thai rod puppets were

A modern, large Thai rod puppet made in the manner of a *hun yai* or *hun laung*, big or royal puppet. *Courtesy the Museum of Cultural History, UCLA. (Photo by Alan G. Cook)*

sometimes highly stylized and sometimes remarkably and beautifully realistic.

The oldest type of rod puppet is known as either *hun yai* (big puppets) or *hun luang* (royal puppets). There is some speculation that this style had its origins in the Ayudhya period of Thai history (1350–1569) but there is no direct evidence for its existence before 1822. According to a literary manuscript called the *Bunnovad*, *hun yai* performances were particularly popular between 1822 and 1843 during the reign of King Boromakot.

Like the *nang talung*, early *hun yai* performances closely resembled the *Khon*—a traditional form of Thai dance/theater. The stories and the music were virtually the same, the costumes were quite similar, and even the removable masks of the *Khon* dancers were retained—in miniature—in the *hun yai*. Great care was taken with the articulation and stringing of the puppets so that they could duplicate the movements of the *Khon* dancers.

A long stick protruded from the bottom to serve as a handle for the manipulator. Strings attached to the limbs and organs and passing through eyelets on the stick down to the manipulator, served to activate the puppets.[8]

During the late 1870s and early 1880s, Chinese puppet shows performed by highly trained Thai courtiers were routinely presented in the palace of Prince Bovorn Vichaicharn, the Vice-Regent of King Rama V. These Chinese-style shows were similar to the traditional royal puppet performances except that Prince Vichaicharn's figures were only about one foot tall—as opposed to the three-foot-high royal puppets. While these newer puppets never developed into a major form—only one set of them was ever made—they did serve to introduce and popularize the use of smaller and more easily manageable rod figures.

Many different styles of these more flexible rod puppets spread from the palace of Vichaicharn into the countryside where they suited the needs of a repertoire that was based primarily on broad comedy and farce. The various rod puppet forms eventually merged into a single style and, late in the nineteenth century, the *hun krabok* puppet came into being.

A *hun krabok* figure had a bamboo torso to which was attached arms and a head. A large, loose-fitting robe covered the entire figure so that, while the head and the hands were visible to the audience, the rods that activated the hands were concealed beneath the robe. Such puppets were much easier to manipulate than the old royal puppets.

While the *hun krabok* was gaining popularity, the one-foot-high rod puppets used by Prince Vichaicharn were revitalized, changed slightly, and called *lakhon lek*. These figures, although similar in appearance to those of Vichaicharn, were much simpler mechanically. The system of internal stringing was eliminated and the puppets were manipulated solely by rods.

While numerous examples of all these various Thai rod puppet styles exist in collections throughout the world, only the *hun krabok* and *lakhon lek* are still regularly performed.

Evidently, the major Thai rod puppet shows—*hun yai, hun krabok,* and *lakhon lek*—utilized similar stages. At any rate, both Monti Tramote and J. Tilakasiri describe only the *lakhon lek* stage.

The Thai puppet stage was almost a replica of the human stage and showed a high degree of ability and skill in its structure. The back and sides of the stage were completely covered to prevent anybody having access inside. Scenery had both its functional and decorative uses. The backdrop hanging about half a yard from the front of the stage contained decorative scenery. Above the backdrop was draped a long strip of cloth decorated with Chinese designs in a gold braid. At the front of the stage and in front of the backdrop a series of glass panels bearing various scenes and illustrations served the purpose of hiding the hands of the operators from the gaze of the audience. Thus everything that appeared within the confined area of the puppet stage—puppets, operators, singers, chorus and musicians—was not visible to the audience.[9]

The earliest Thai rod puppet theater performances were musically sophisticated and highly literate events that catered to the refined tastes of the Thai aristocracy. However, by the early years of the twentieth century, broad farce and comic byplay were becoming increasingly important in both the *hun krabok* and *lakhon lek* performances. Finally, with the overthrow of the Thai monarchy in 1932, the rod puppet show lost its most important devotees and patrons.

Thailand is still in the process of complicated political and social change. What effect this process of change will have on its traditional arts of shadow and rod puppetry is impossible to determine. It seems likely, however, that the *nang talung, hun krabok* and *lakhon lek* will endure for present and future audiences.

CAMBODIA

The two forms of shadow puppet theater that survive in Cambodia are similar to the *nang yai* and *nang talung* of Thailand. The Cambodian giant shadow play is called either *nang sbek* or *nang sbek luong*. These figures are held aloft by dancers/puppeteers who appear in front of the shadow screen. The steps, leaps, and poses of the puppeteers are clearly derived from those of the Cambodian Royal Ballet. The dance movements for each of the one hundred and fifty or so characters "have been meticulously laid down and are varied according to the characters and the situations in which they find themselves. The accompanying music is also varied according to the type of character and to mood."[10] The stories are drawn from the *Ream Ker*, the Cambodian *Ramayana*.

The smaller Cambodian shadow figures are called *nang ayang* or *nang kaloung* and resemble the Thai's *nang talung*. The subjects of the *nang ayang* plays are drawn either from Buddhist legends or from the *Ream Ker*. Tilakasiri notes that: "Giants, demons, monkeys as well as minor deities like divine nymphs *(apsaras)* and spirits appearing at frequent intervals enhance the visual appeal of the show. The puppet figures are so designed that they can easily be used for several stories."[11] According to tradition, male characters are carved in profile while female characters usually face front. Like the *nang talung*, the *nang kaloung* are remarkably realistic.

Music for the shadow puppet performances is set by tradition:

> The musical accompaniment . . . is provided by the *pinpeat* orchestra which consists of two *sralay,* two xylophones, two sets of circular gongs, a horizontal drum and two large kettle drums. There are set tunes for four different situations called procession, combat, sorrow or pain and transformation.[12]

A *sralay* is an oboelike instrument with six finger-holes.

As might be expected in this region, the element of modern militarism has crept into the shadow shows, and modern clothing, military uniforms, automobiles, and airplanes sometimes appear.

It is uncertain to what extent either the *nang sbek* or the *nang kaloung* survive in Cambodia. Certainly they still exist, but only as holdovers from a former and less devastatingly war-torn age.

MALAYSIA

The northeastern province of Kelantan is the center of Malaysia's puppet activity. Shadow puppetry, the only major form in the region, was probably imported from Java during the eighteenth century.

As in Java, the entire shadow puppet performance is under the direction of a *dalang*, who serves as puppeteer, director, and orchestra leader. The Malaysian orchestra consists of gongs, bells, drums, a stringed instrument known as a *rebab*, and a clarinetlike instrument called a *seruma*. This orchestra, like the Javanese *gamelan*, accompanies the whole show, punctuating and underscoring the major moods and actions of the play.

There are three varieties of Malayan shadow puppets. The *wayang diawa* is Javanese in form and performance style; its figures are highly stylized and have two movable arms. The *wayang melaya* are realistically shaped and usually have only one movable arm. The subject matter of both these forms is drawn from the *Ramayana*, the *Mahabharata*, the Javanese Panji plays, and the Islamic stories based on the adventures of the Indonesian hero Amir Hamzah. The third type, the *wayang siam*, is the most popular of the three forms, with figures that are intricately cut and painted to resemble the Thai *Khon*, the masked, classical dance.

Tilakasiri observes that in most respects:

The Malayan shadow play has borrowed the style, techniques and procedures traditionally employed in the Javanese style performance. The play is preceded by the religious and ritualistic preliminaries associated with the presentation of the plays in Java.[13]

Shadow performances are usually commissioned for important social and religious events. On these occasions, plays are presented serially every night for one week. On the first six nights the presentation ends at about midnight but on the seventh it lasts until dawn. These performances are enlivened by the misadventures of two traditional clowns who seem to go by a variety of names; the first is known as Semar or Pa' Dogol and the second as Turis, Chemuris, or Wa'Long.

Although shadow plays are no longer performed in the cities of Malaysia, the shadow show continues to be popular in the villages of Kelantan, where it remains an important part of social and religious life.

VIETNAM

Vietnam's traditional puppets are particularly spectacular and unusual. Known as *water puppets*, the figures are suspended over water and controlled by an odd combination of rods and strings.

A special structure closely resembling a Vietnamese communal house is built in the middle of a lake. It is used to house the puppets and the operators. After the audience gathers, the show is briefly introduced by a concealed orchestra that makes loud and liberal use of gongs and cymbals.

A fascinating eyewitness account by Lorraine Salmon of a water puppet performance is included in *Puppet Theatre Around the World*. Ms. Salmon notes that the performance began with fireworks in which firecrackers, attached to small pieces of wood, were thrown onto the surface of the lake. After a particularly loud explosion, small flags outlining the stage were raised from beneath the surface of the water. Then, a number of interesting puppets depicting scenes from Vietnamese village life appeared:

> There were the peasants plowing with a great water buffalo, or leading the docile oxen. Women weeded the fields, searched for snails, or sat at home and spun or wove cloth. They were visited by gossiping neighbors and a scolding mother-in-law. A minute baby was shown off by a proud mother. Groups of dancers solemnly took the stage and gyrated with the formal movements of the Vietnamese dance. A group of acrobats climbed onto each other's shoulders, or clambered up greasy poles, or performed on high ladders. . . .
>
> On to the watery stage came a marionette fisherman, with a great square net, sprung on bamboo. Around him cheekily gambolled small and huge fish, refusing to be caught. The orchestra crashed and banged and voices behind the curtain told the stories. . . .
>
> From above the stage a model aeroplane appeared and swooped around the sky. And whose figures were those in the watery fields below? Men of the Vietnam People's Army, of course, who with the most skillful use of fireworks, shot their guns into the air and brought the plane down in flames.[14]

The battle continued with a complete array of modern war machines including a large battleship that was skillfully maneuvered into a fierce battle with an unseen adversary. At a crucial point, the fabled monsters of Vietnam come to the aid of the people.

> Dragons, many feet long and cunningly jointed, were joined by a phoenix, its long neck swaying gracefully as it moved over the watery stage. . . . Suddenly in their midst appeared foreign soldiers who soon found themselves set upon by dragons and phoenix alike. To the triumphant rolls of drums and crashings of cymbals, the invaders were defeated and disappeared under the waves. The dragons and the phoenix resumed their happy guardianship of Vietnam, the show was over. . . .[15]

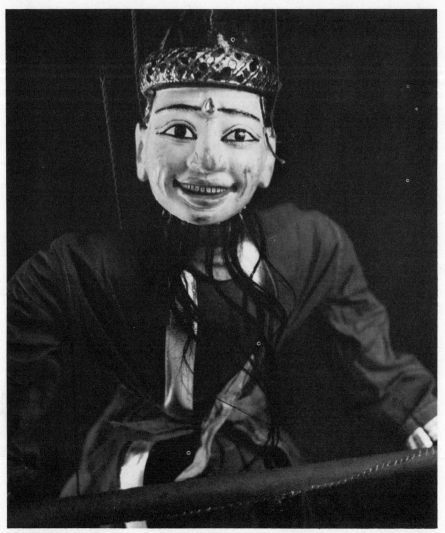

Burmese marionette. *Courtesy the Museum of Cultural History, UCLA. (Photo by Alan G. Cook)*

Photographs of Vietnamese water puppets can be found in *Puppet Theatre Around the World*[16] and *The Puppet Theatre of the Modern World*[17] as well as in an article on Vietnamese puppetry by Leh Vinh Tuyh which appeared in a 1965 edition of *World Theatre*.[18]

The three-dimensional, brightly painted, wooden water puppet figures are from two and a half to three feet high. The puppeteers manipulate their figures with the aid of long bamboo poles that are equipped with a special network of strings.

The village of Nguyen Xa is the traditional home of Vietnamese water puppetry. Under the Communist regime, water puppetry is apparently experiencing a new popularity. Reportedly, there are now hundreds of puppet companies all over Vietnam. Some of them are run by professionals but most are under the control of skilled amateurs. Despite this popularity, Vietnamese water puppets are extremely difficult to find outside of Vietnam. Many Western puppeteers and puppet theater historians look forward to a time when first-hand information on the unique, traditional water puppet theater of Vietnam will be more readily available.

BURMA

The traditional style of Burmese puppetry was developed by U Thaw, the Minister of Royal Entertainment in the court of Nga-Sanit Gu Min during the final quarter of the eighteenth century. Although most of the folk arts of Burma show strong Indian and Siamese influence, the *yoke thay*, as the marionette theater is called, is entirely Burmese in its style and story matter.

Developed for members of the Burmese court, the *yoke thay* was, from its beginnings, an elaborate and highly sophisticated form of entertainment. In addition, the puppet theater was a successful way of avoiding the moral strictures against unmarried men and women appearing together on the same stage.

It is worth nothing that some Burmese historians believe that the *yoke thay* preceded and set the style for the development of the live Burmese court drama or *zat*. As a result, early *zat* actors and dancers were often evaluated on the basis of how well or poorly they duplicated the difficult and complicated movements of the *yoke thay*.

The plots and themes of the *yoke thay* plays were based upon the *Jataka*—the five hundred and fifty birth stories of the Buddha—or upon significant events in Burmese history. The puppet figures vary in height from two and a half to three feet. Some of the characters have as many as sixty strings.

The number of figures in a traditional *yoke thay* set is a matter for some obviously and amusingly inaccurate opinion.

Tilakasiri says that:

The traditional marionette show of Burma possesses 27 figures, viz., two nat votaresses, one horse, two elephants (one white, the other black), a tiger, a monkey, two parrots, one necromancer, four ministers, a King, a prince, a princess, two prince-regents (one white-faced and the other red-faced), an astrologer, a hermit, a nat, a

A Burmese marionette prince. *Courtesy Ellen Proctor. (Photo by David L. Young)*

maha-deva, an old man and two buffoons. These 27 figures constituting the full cast of a show has been known to exist from the beginning of the marionette tradition, but later on other figures were added.[19]

It should be noted that Tilakasiri's addition is wrong. He lists

132

A Burmese horse made in the late 1950s. *Courtesy Alan G. Cook. (Photo by Alan G. Cook)*

twenty-six and not twenty-seven figures. But U Tha Myat, former director of the Cultural Institute in Ragoon was even worse at arithmetic:

> A traditional marionette show has 28 figures, comprised of 2 nat votaresses, a horse, 2 elephants (black and white), a tiger, a monkey, a parrot, 2 ogres, a jogi, 4 ministers, a King, a prince, 2 prince-regents, an astrologer, a hermit, an old woman and 2 clowns. Some shows have more figures, but the traditional company of marionettes is one of 28 figures only.[20]

U Tha Myat's twenty-eight add up to twenty-four.

The *yoke thay* puppeteers are concealed behind a special backcloth that is hung at the rear of a raised bamboo platform. The Burmese puppet theater utilizes scenery such as a monastery, a palace, a throne, a carriage, a pagoda, and a forest—which is usually nothing more than a few small, leafy branches.

A centrally placed tree divides the marionette stage into two parts. Good characters such as elephants, kings, and ministers inhabit the right side of the stage and evil characters such as the tiger, the old man, and the necromancer inhabit the left. While most of the characters enter behind the back screen, the monkeys and certain other characters are often raised and lowered directly from the bridge; this is the conventional manner of suggesting that these characters are capable of jumping and/or flying great distances.

As in many parts of Asia, performances lasted all night. A traditional performance was divided into two distinct sections. The first section detailed the creation of the world and made a great show of animals, ogres, and spirits, their friendships and enmities. The second section was about the kingdoms of men on earth and was largely concerned with kings, princes, and courtiers, and the relationships between them. During the nineteenth century, the plays were very popular among the Burmese aristocracy, and individual performances often became subtle instruments of political suggestion and persuasion.

There are still a few companies who perform the old *yoke thay* plays in something like the traditional manner, particularly in the area around Mandalay. In general, however, the art of Burmese string puppetry is in decline and is not likely to survive the often merciless processes that pass for progress in the twentieth century.

NOTES

1. J. Tilakasiri, *The Puppet Theatre of Asia* (Ceylon: Dept. of Cultural Affairs, 1968), p. 39.
2. Euayporn Kerdchouay and Michael Smithies. "Giant Shadow Play of Thailand." *Orientations* (August 1973), p. 47.
3. Ibid.
4. Tilakasiri, *The Puppet Theatre of Asia*, p. 40.
5. Kerdchouay and Smithies, "Giant Shadow Play of Thailand," p. 48.
6. Ibid., p. 49.
7. Tilakasiri, *The Puppet Theatre of Asia*, p. 40.
8. Monti Tramote. "Thai Puppet Shows," *Puppet Theatre Around the World,* ed. Som Benegal (Bharatya Natya Sangh: New Delhi, 1960), p. 60.
9. Tilakasiri, *The Puppet Theatre of Asia*, p. 42.
10. Ibid., p. 45.
11. Ibid.
12. Ibid.
13. Ibid., p. 46.
14. Lorraine Salmon. "Water Puppets of Vietnam," *Puppet Theatre Around the World,* p. 114.
15. Ibid., p. 116.
16. Ibid.
17. *The Puppet Theatre of the Modern World,* ed. by Margareta Niculescu, Plays Inc., Boston, 1967, Plates 209–14.
18. Leh Vinh Tuyh. "Vietnam's Terrestrial and Aquatic Puppets," *World Theatre* (vol. 14, no. 5 (1965), p. 12.
19. Tilakasiri, *The Puppet Theatre of Asia*, p. 37.
20. U Tha Myat, "Puppet Show of Burna," *Puppet Theatre Around the World,* p. 43.

8

Japan and Korea
Puppetry as Classical and Folk Theater

JAPAN

The earliest Japanese word for puppet was *kugutsu* and the first documented use of it dates from the eighth century A.D. Scholars have noted that *kugutsu* bears an intriguing similarity to ancient, non-Japanese words for puppet. The Chinese word, for example, was *kuai-luai-tzu,* the Gypsy term was *kuki* or *kukli,* the Turkish word was *kukla,* and the somewhat more recent Greek word was *koukla.* Some scholars believe that these similarities constitute evidence that puppetry began in Asia Minor and then spread across Asia to India, Southeast Asia, China, Korea, and, finally, to Japan.[1]

Others note that the sounds *kugu* and *kugutsu* often appear in the names of ancient Japanese shrines and gods, a fact that signifies a possible relationship between puppets and the conduct of religious ceremonies at certain Shinto shrines. Donald Keene suggests that:

Puppets preserved today at shrines in scattered areas of Japan clearly suggest ancient traditions behind them. In the north, the worship of the god Oshira, involves a medium who recites spells and stories accompanied by the two simple stick puppets she operates, one in each hand, raising, lowering, or confronting the puppets as she speaks. At two shrines in Kyushu, puppets, perhaps the oldest in Japan, perform dances and wrestling matches as part of the annual festival. These Shinto puppets are not representations of divinities (in the manner of Buddhist or Christian images) but, rather, wooden creatures temporarily "possessed" by the gods whose actions they recreate, much as the medium herself is believed to repeat, when possessed, words uttered by the god himself.[2]

135

The earliest description of Japanese puppeteers dates from the eleventh century. It suggests that they were a nomadic and somewhat disreputable lot. The men were hunters as well as entertainers and the women were often prostitutes. The performances of these puppeteers—also known as *kugutsu*—were evidently coarse and full of violent action.

During the fourteenth century, the introduction of marionettes from China brought new popularity and a high level of technical sophistication to Japanese puppetry. By the middle of the fifteenth century, puppets were occasionally used to present miniaturized versions of the austere, classical *Noh* dramas, as well as for the irreverent interludes between the acts of a *Noh* play that were known as *kyogen* farces. In the middle of the sixteenth century, puppeteers regularly presented plays in honor of the god Ebisu at his shrine in Nishinomiya and, eventually, the word *ebisu* came to mean "puppet." By the late seventeenth century, the term *ebisu-mai* referred to a type of string puppet show in which the marionettes were about eight inches high and were manipulated on portable stages. These theaters were slung around the necks of the puppeteers and were made to resemble small *Noh* stages.

A Buddhist hand puppet form known as *hotoke mawashi* developed during the seventeenth century at about the same time as the *ebisu-mai*. The *hotoke mawashi* strongly influenced the development of the *sekkyo-bushi,* which was a type of morality play performed with puppets. In the late seventeenth century, the *sekkyo-bushi* became quite popular.[3]

There were at least three other types of little-known Japanese puppet traditions. The *kami-shibai* is a paper theater in which cut-out figures move in grooves while the puppeteer recites the dialogue.[4] The form evidently bears certain stylistic similarities to the English toy theater. The second type of figure is the *karuma* puppet. "Found in the villages around Tokyo, the *karuma* puppet is operated by a single performer who sits on a small wagon with the puppet. The head of the puppet is controlled by the left hand and the puppet's right arm is controlled by the operator's right arm. The legs of the figure are controlled by the legs of the puppeteer."[5] The third type, the *noroma* puppet, has been described in the following way: ". . . Japanese term meaning 'stupid' puppet, applied to a primitive type found on Sado Island and controlled by the performer's hands around the puppet body."[6]

Despite the past and present popularity of so many kinds of puppetry in Japan, there is one form that has received more specific attention from scholars than any of the others. This form has come to be called

Five Bunraku heads. Note the stringing mechanisms for operating the facial features. *Courtesy Alan G. Cook. (Photo by Alan G. Cook)*

Bunraku, and along with *Noh* and *Kabuki,* it is generally regarded as one of the three major forms of classical Japanese theater.

The unique style that has made *Bunraku* so famous can be traced to the sixteenth century when professional chanters began to recite elaborate, romantic ballads to the accompaniment of a stringed instrument called the *biwa.* Because the most popular of these ballads was called *The Tale in Twelve Episodes of Joruri,* the form itself eventually became known as *joruri.* While *joruri* was developing during the seventeenth century, the *samisen,* a stringed instrument originally from China, was substituted for the *biwa.* The art of *joruri* was first combined with puppetry around 1600 when *ebisu-kaki* puppeteers were invited to provide visual accompaniment to the songs and chants of some *joruri* performers. This new form became known as *ningyo-joruri—ningyo* being a Japanese word for doll or puppet.

The first great theater devoted to the art of *ningyo-joruri* was opened in 1685 by Takemoto Gidayu (1650–1714). With his friend, the influential Japanese playwright Chikematsu Monzaemon, and the other artists of his theater, he strove to create a finely controlled blend

Japanese paper puppets such as this one are stiffened internally with thin pieces of wood. *Courtesy Melvyn Helstien. (Photo by Alan G. Cook)*

of the skills of the narrator, the puppeteers, and the *samisen* player. Later artists continued to develop the elaborate traditions of *ningyo-joruri* performance. In 1734, for example, it was decided that each of the major puppets should be operated by three men. Eventually, a first and master puppeteer was made responsible for the manipulation of the figure's head and right arm; a second puppeteer for the left arm as well as for all hand properties; and a third puppeteer operated the legs and feet. In order to heighten the illusion that the puppet was walking on solid ground, the third puppeteer stamped his feet on special

138

Japanese paper puppet. *Courtesy Melvyn Helstien. (Photo by Alan G. Cook)*

wooden planks as the figure moved about the stage. Although female puppets were made without legs, the third operator suggested their presence by cleverly manipulating the hem of the puppet's kimono. This difficult and distinctive style of manipulation is still used.

From about 1715 until about 1795, the *ningyo-joruri* was much more popular than the *Kabuki,* which is a live theater form with elaborate costumes, makeup, and a great deal of music and dance. At the turn of the nineteenth century, the *Kabuki* theaters fought back, adapting the puppet plays for their own uses. They achieved spectacular scenic, costuming, and acting effects that the puppet theater could not hope to match. During the nineteenth century, the *ningyo-joruri* once again became extremely popular, but it never regained the extraordinary position of prominence that it held in the eighteenth century.

The term *Bunraku* was not commonly used until the late nineteenth

Figure of a Bunraku lady. *Courtesy of Alan G. Cook (Photo by Alan G. Cook)*

century. The word is derived from the name Uemura Bunrakuken, who was a famous *ningyo-joruri* artist and entrepreneur of the late eighteenth century. He, his descendants, and followers had so much to do with the re-emergence of Japan's puppet theater that by the last quarter of the nineteenth century the word *Bunraku* became the popular and generally accepted term for *ningyo-joruri*.

The *Bunraku* figures themselves are quite large, although minor roles such as attendants or maids are represented by smaller dolls called *tsume*, which are operated by one person. Male puppets are often three-quarters life size while female figures are slightly smaller. Some of the puppets have articulated eyes, mouths, eyebrows, and fingers. The heads are carved and painted with exquisite subtlety and precision. Costuming is sumptuous and reveals painstaking devotion to historical tradition and detail.

The heads, whether articulated or not, are works of art in themselves. They are carved by a very small number of master craftsmen out of cypress or paulownia wood. The solid head is then sawed in half and hollowed out. If it is to have moveable parts, the necessary mechanisms are set in place before the head is glued back together. Finally, it is covered with as many as fourteen or fifteen coats of paint—a process that gives the head a delicate, porcelainlike finish.

The head grip of a *Bunraku* puppet fits into a hole in a roughly shaped shoulder board. The lower arms and lower legs as well as a bamboo hoop that represents the hips are suspended on strings from the appropriate parts of this board. Additional special padding is sometimes used for characters with unusual body types. Several strings that control the facial mechanisms are attached to the handgrip, which the chief puppeteer holds with his right hand. This hand is inserted through a special opening in the costume at the back of the figure.

The beauty of the puppets is matched by the diversity of their uses. The Japanese author Shuzaburo Hronaga notes that:

> There are 45 kinds of dolls' heads in common use in the puppet theatre, including eight for old men, eighteen for middle-aged men, five for young men and children, three for old women, four for middle-aged women, and seven for young women.[7]

Each head is used to portray a number of different roles in different plays. For each role, the hair is styled in a particular way and used with an appropriately costumed body. Sometimes, several heads representing varying moods of the same character will be used for one role. Duplicate heads are placed on differently costumed bodies in order to facilitate rapid changes of costume.

The most respected members of a *Bunraku* troupe are the narrators. A boy begins his training for this job at the age of ten by becoming an apprentice to an already established narrator. In this position, he is expected to learn the literature of the art as well as to practice all of the techniques of breath control and vocal conditioning that are the basic elements of the narrator's art.

The narrator's rhythms, moods, and pitches must be meticulously and rigorously set so that the puppeteers and *samisen* players can operate with precision and unity. His manner of delivery is a highly stylized combination of chanting, singing, and acting:

> It is the *joruri* reciter who is mainly responsible for creating atmosphere in the play. If the scene is a town house, he begins his recitation briskly; serenely if it is a farm house; gaily if it is a tea house; eerily if it is in a forest. In emotional passages, he may turn purple in the face, sweat profusely, spit, roll his eyes and shed genuine tears. He must not only be able to carry his tone in speaking the dialogue of contrasting male characters, but he must have at his command a tolerable falsetto for the female parts.[8]

While on stage, the narrator performs all of the roles and provides all of the commentary. Because his task is so strenuous, two or more narrators are normally required for a complete performance.

During the show, the narrator sits on a platform that is built out into the audience on the stage left side of the puppet stage. In front of him, on a small stand, he holds the text. Behind him sits the *samisen* player. The platform on which they all sit is a turntable, and at certain points in the performance, it is turned one hundred and eighty degrees so that, without breaking rhythm or continuity, the narrator and *samisen* player can be whisked out of sight and replaced with new performers for the next section of the play.

The narrator and the *samisen* player work together as an intricately cooperating team. The music of the *samisen* reinforces the vocal tones and rhythms that are set by the narrator. Ultimately, the *samisen* music expresses and augments all the emotional and dramatic effects of a *Bunraku* performance:

> The *samisen* provides not only a musical accompaniment to the *joruri* recitation, but also an indication, where appropriate, of the sound of rain or wind or other effect to heighten the atmosphere of the scene. It must lead or drive as the case may be, the voice of the reciter with such a sequence and with such a sound as to describe exactly the particular situation or mood at the very moment. At appropriate moments of dramatic tension, there emerge strenuous chords, stirring rhythmical crescendos or falling glissandos like dying wails.[9]

In performance, the puppeteers as well as the narrator and *samisen* players are always in full view of the audience. The puppeteers stand behind a partition that reaches to the waist of the chief puppeteer. It forms a long alleyway with the audience in front and the painted stage

Bunraku figure of a young man. *Courtesy Margo Lovelace. (Photo by Davi Young)*

scenery at the rear. If there is scenery in the foreground it is held by assistants or supported on a special stand. Since much of the background scenery is suspended on a system of movable lines and pulleys, rapid scene changes can be managed with relative ease. Despite the fact that the performers remain in full view of the spectators, their extraordinary artistry makes it easy for the audience to concentrate on the movements of the puppets. In fact, according to most observors, after a few minutes, it becomes virtually impossible not to concentrate on the puppets.

The principal puppeteers, as well as the narrators and *samisen* players, wear a simplified version of a *samurai* costume with stiff protruding shoulder pieces worn over an unadorned *kimono*. The two junior puppeteers are dressed entirely in black. Their faces are covered by a black hood over a wire frame. Smooth operation of the figures requires that the principal puppeteer stand higher than his two assistants. In order to accomplish this, he wears high, light, hollow wooden clogs, while his assistants wear simple slippers.

Until the 1920s, the training process for a puppeteer was severe and time consuming. An apprentice began training at about the age of ten, eventually attaining the status of third puppeteer—an operator of the feet. After another ten years, he could become an operator of the left arm and finally—after yet another ten years—if he was talented and lucky, he became a principal puppeteer. The reason usually given for this long period of apprenticeship is that the art of manipulation is so difficult that it requires thirty years to master. Probably, however, this answer is only a partial one. More than likely, master puppeteers were understandably reluctant to break up successful three-man teams that had been so carefully and arduously trained over a period of several years.

Bunraku puppeteers take pride in their observance of performance traditions. Donald Keene has observed that:

> Whatever role an operator assumes, he must observe its traditions, or if a new work, the traditions of similar parts in older works of the repertory. In addition, he is bound by the traditional appearance of the puppets.[10]

Even the specific gestures of the figures are most often dictated by tradition. *Bunraku* puppeteers distinguish two types of gesture or movement. Examples of the first type are known as *furi*. These are stylized methods of representing normal human actions, such as sewing, eating, weeping, laughing, and so forth. The second type of gesture is known as *kata*. These gestures are used to reveal the peculiar

Modern Bunraku figure of a knight wears elaborate gold brocaded costume and has articulated eyes, eyebrows, wrists, and neck. *Courtesy Detroit Museum of Arts, Theatre Dept, (Photo by David L. Young)*

beauty and grace of the puppets themselves.[11] The operators strive to create psychologically true characters and an aesthetically pleasing performance as well as clarity in terms of mood, meaning, and character relationships.

Gestures performed by actors can be so restrained as to be almost unperceptible (sic) at times, yet retain their effect because of the unifying strength of the actor's personality. In the puppet theatre, however, the inability of the puppets to rival the subtlety of the movement of a living person has led the operators to choose the opposite extreme: they create the illusion of life by simplifying and intensifying human gestures so as to make the audience feel it is witnessing a distillation of the emotions experienced by the characters on the stage. Nothing, then, can be casual or approximate; a repertory of clearly defined gestures is employed to define each movement.[12]

The complexity of the puppeteers' art must be understood in the light of the fact that each gesture, no matter how large or small, is produced by three men who have learned to work together as one.

Most of the plays in the *Bunraku* repertory date from either the seventeenth or the eighteenth century and are one of two types. Those of the type called *jidai mono* concern the lives, loves, and adventures of great warriors and powerful aristocrats. The plays of the type known as *sewanomo* deal with the romantic and moral problems of the middle and merchant classes in eighteenth century Japan. By modern standards, both types of plays are quite long and complicated. Nowadays, these dramas, which usually stress the ideals of loyalty to superiors and devotion to a strict traditional moral code, are rarely performed in their entirety. Usually, either an individual act from one play or a series of intensely dramatic scenes from various plays are performed instead. Although few people, whether Japanese or foreign, fail to appreciate the technical mastery of the *Bunraku* artists, the fact is that, with the exception of a relatively small number of scholars and enthusiasts, the general public is no longer attracted to the theater in large numbers. This is true even on the Japanese islands of Sado and Awaji, where similar, although far less sophisticated forms of *Bunraku* still survive.

Most probably, the *Bunraku's* strong reliance on traditional methods and modes of performance is both its chief asset and its major liability. On the one hand, because each play and gesture has been rehearsed and performed for centuries, the form often attains a technical mastery and beauty that is clearly the product of a time-consuming and arduously sought perfection. On the other hand, through its heavy reliance on past traditions that appealed to the middle classes of a former age, the art has almost completely lost touch with present-day audiences. There is no continuing tradition of new plays that might infuse new spirit into the old forms, and younger generations of Japanese puppeteers have lost patience with the old methods of prolonged training. Because it is generally regarded as something of a national cultural and historical resource, *Bunraku* will survive for some time to come. But it will take modern geniuses with the discipline, abilities, and energy of the *ningyo-joruri*'s first great innovator and producer, Takemoto Gidayu, and first great playwright, Chikematsu Monzaemon, to repopularize the form for a modern Japan that nonetheless venerates its remarkable and magnificent puppet theater, the *Bunraku*.

KOREA

There are only two styles of Korean puppetry that can be classified as genuine folk theater forms and both of them are now virtually extinct. The first was the primitive *Man-seog-jung* play. The second, and more important of the two, was known by two names: the *ggogdu gagsi* play or the *Bag Cheomji* play.

Until the early 1930s, the *Man-seog-jung* play was traditionally performed on the feast of Buddha's birthday. *Man-seog-jung*, the main character, was always dressed in a Buddhist ceremonial coat and cap. This puppet was a three-dimensional figure made from wood and dried gourds. According to available descriptions, it was similar to the jumping-jack figures that have amused generations of children around the world:

> Two holes are bored in the chest of the *Man-seog-jung* puppet, through which four strings are passed and tied to both hands and legs so that the hands can be pulled up to its chest and the legs can hit its head as the player behind the puppet pulls the strings.[13]

Flat cardboard puppets of a stag and a roe deer as well as colorful paper figures of a dragon and a carp completed the cast of puppet characters in the *Man-seog-jung* play. The performance was as much a traditional holiday display as it was a puppet show.

The origins of the *ggogdu gagsi* or *Bag Cheomji* play are lost in antiquity. It was, however, quite common through the 1940s. By the late 1950s and early 1960s it was artificially preserved through the efforts of Dr. Choe Sang-su and the Korean Folklore Society who sponsored a small number of public performances. As is the case with

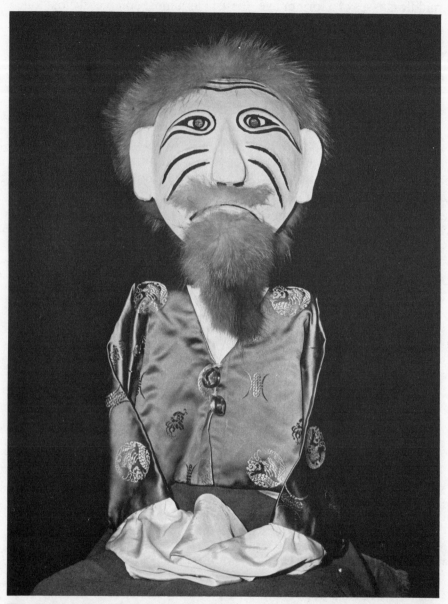

This Korean *Bag Cheomji* puppet with a movable mouth is approximately twenty-four inches high. The figure's head is a gourd, painted in flesh tones. The hair and beard are of animal fur. *Courtesy Don Avery and the Puppet Guild of St. Louis. (Photo: Photographic by Steve)*

most scholarly attempts to revive a popular art, their efforts were doomed before they began.

In its heyday, the play was usually performed for and by farmers. A company was made up of six or seven men who were farmers as well as semiprofessional performers. Only three or four members of the group were puppeteers. The rest were musicians who accompanied the performances with an hourglass-shaped drum known as the *jang-go,* a brass hand gong called the *gawaeng-gwari,* and a simple wooden reed instrument known as a *nallari* or *hojeog.*

The players traveled from village to village performing on threshing grounds or in marketplaces. The stage was constructed by stretching a wide piece of cloth around four poles that were set into the ground. The playing area that was formed in this way was approximately six and a half feet square and six feet high. Concealed within this screened area, the players made their string and rod figures speak, dance, and sing above the top edge of the theater. Some of the voices had a high-pitched, reedy quality that was produced with the aid of a special bamboo pipe through which the puppeteers would speak. The figures themselves were usually between twenty and forty inches high and were made from gourds, wood, fabric, and fur.

The puppeteer manipulated a *Bag Cheomji* puppet by using one hand to grasp and turn a rectangular control rod that extended from the base of the puppet to its head. With his other hand, the puppeteer pulled strings that were attached to the figure's mouth and arms. Under the control of an expert operator, who could move the mouth and arms with great skill, the puppet also seemed to have hands, although, in fact, it had none.

The *Bag Cheomji* shows lasted about an hour and were performed at night by torchlight. They dealt with the adventures and misadventures of the elderly farmer Bag Cheomji and his family. The Korean scholar Choe Sang-su divided the play into eight loosely related episodes. With the exception of the scene in which Bag Cheomji outwits the voracious monster, Yeongo, all of the episodes depict scenes and situations drawn from Korean country life: an adventure in an inn, a family reunion in a Buddhist temple, a squabble between Bag Cheomji's wife and his concubine, a snake bite emergency in the fields, an encounter with a provincial governor hunting with his hawk, a funeral, and the building of a Buddhist temple.

The entire play required sixteen characters: Bag Cheomji, his wife, his concubine, his younger brother, his niece, his niece-in-law, his nephew, four temple attendants, the governor, the governor's assistant, the hunter, the monster, and the villager/musician.

Today, there are only one or two Bag Cheomji companies in

existence. According to Choe Sang-su, towards the end of the nineteenth century "western civilization rushed into Korea and the people gradually learned to love the new culture and their enthusiasm about the old culture cooled and puppetry was subject to the law of natural selection."[14] Without question, it is easy to understand how the people of a modernized, westernized, divided, and war-torn nation such as Korea, could lose touch with a theatrical form that was created for the less complicated tastes of their ancestors. But no matter how outmoded a tradition may seem, its passing is always regretted by those who understand its cultural significance.

NOTES

1. Donald Keene. *Bunraku: The Art of the Japanese Puppet Theatre* (Palo Alto: Kodansha International Press, 1965), p. 19.
2. Ibid.
3. Ibid., p. 24.
4. A. R. Philpott. *Dictionary of Puppetry* (Boston: Plays, Inc., 1965), p. 128.
5. Ibid., p. 132.
6. Ibid., p. 170.
7. Shuzaburo Hironaga. *Bunraku: Japan's Unique Puppet Theatre* (Tokyo: Tokyo News Service, 1964), p. 6.
8. Ibid., p. 3.
9. Ibid.
10. Keene, *Bunraku: The Art of the Japanese Puppet Theatre*, p. 52.
11. Ibid., p. 57.
12. Ibid., p. 56.
13. Choe Sang-Su, *A Study of the Korean Puppet Play* (Seoul: The Korean Book Publishing Co., 1961), p. 4.
14. Ibid., p. 56.

9

Puppets of the Pacific
The New Hebrides, Easter Island,
and Hawaii

Despite the rich heritage of masks and carved figures throughout the many cultures of the Pacific Islands, only three forms of puppetry have been documented. One such form existed until the first quarter of this century on the islands of the New Hebrides. Another form—long since extinct—is known to have been popular among the former inhabitants of Easter Island. A third form existed in the Hawaiian Islands until the late nineteenth century.

The most complete information concerning the primitive *temes nevinbur* puppets of the New Hebrides can be found in Bernard Deacon's book *Malekula: A Vanishing People in the New Hebrides*, published in London in 1934. Important additional material can be found in Francoise Girard's essay "Un Theâtre de Marionnettes aux Nouvelles-Hébrides: Son Importance Religieuse," which appeared in a 1956 edition of *New Hebrides Tribus*. It is from these two sources that most of the material concerning the *temes nevinbur* puppets is drawn.

Temes nevinbur is the generic name for two or three different types of puppets that were used until approximately 1925 in a ritual ceremony of an aboriginal tribe inhabiting Malekula, one of the islands of the New Hebrides.

Although these puppets are by no means common, they can be found. Two *temes nevinbur* are displayed in the Musée de l'Homme in Paris and there is another in the Puppet Collection in the City of

Temes Nevinbur **puppet from the New Hebrides. The head is made of a mixture of fiber, wood, and clay.** *Courtesy Fine Arts Museums of San Francisco; M.H. deYoung Memorial Museum.*

Munich. The photograph in this chapter is of a *temes nevinbur* figure in the M. H. deYoung Memorial Museum in San Francisco.

Temes nevinbur puppets are relatively fragile. The heads are modeled from a kind of vegetable paste that is applied over a coconut or a ball of leaves and then mounted on the tip of a bamboo cane or other slender stick. Completed figures are normally about thirty-two inches high and are colored in various shades of black, white, brown, and red. It is impossible to find any of the major characters because at the climax of the performances in which they appeared, they were deliberately destroyed. Fortunately, certain of the minor characters were preserved by a handful of traders, anthropologists, and other visitors to the area.

The features of these extant figures are grotesque, with huge teeth, enormous brow ridges, large mouths, and oversized eyes. There is, in addition, often some kind of headdress made from tufts of bark or hair.

According to Deacon, *nevinbur* is the name of a secret male society that existed in the Seniang district of the island of Malekula in the New Hebrides. Not a great deal is known concerning the legends that were central to the society's beliefs and ceremonies. It is known, however, that the major characters of these legends were Mansip, his two wives, Lieur and Lisivu, his mother-in-law, Nevinbumbau, and his many grandchildren. *Nevinbur* society members believed that their puppets represented mortal souls, or *temes*.

Temes nevinbur figures were used in connection with a secret, ritual ceremony that was performed in a special dancing place. Deacon divides this ceremony into three parts: " . . . the destruction of the grandchildren of Mansip, these effigies being supposed to be rotten; the construction of hundreds of new effigies of these *temes;* and finally, the spearing to death of Mansip and his two wives."[1] The ritual was part of the initiation of members into the secret *nevinbur* society.

The highlight of this ceremony was a primitive puppet play. While the play was in preparation, the women were required to leave the village at dawn and spend the daylight hours in a special house out of sight and hearing of *nevinbur* society members. Within the village, a high wooden fence was built around the *nevinbur* ceremonial house and its adjacent dancing area in order to conceal the activities of members from the prying eyes of the male nonmembers who remained at home.

Just prior to the first stage of the performance, the puppet figures of Mansip and his two wives were placed in a specially constructed shelter outside of the fenced area. This display served to announce the beginning of the play to the audience of women, children, and uninitiated males.

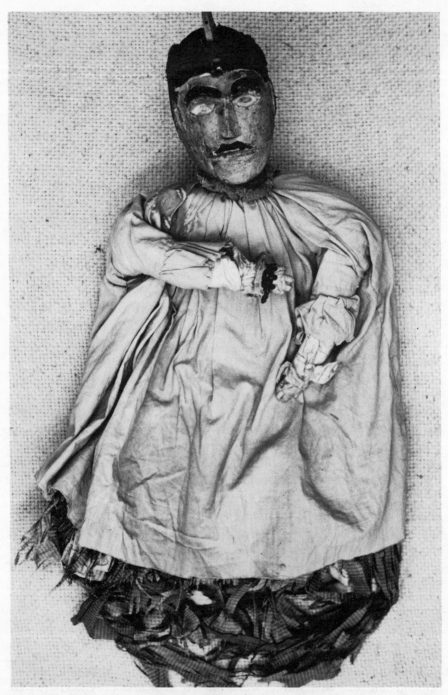

Hula ki'i puppet from Hawaii of the late nineteenth or very early twentieth century. *Courtesy Smithsonian Institution. (Photo by David L. Young*

Deacon indicates something of the care that the *nevinbur* society took to imbue their puppets with the appearance of life:

> A number of bamboos are taken, the nodes of which have been perforated, and are buried in such a way that one end of them appears above ground inside the enclosure . . . the other end reaches the surface inside Mansip's house just behind the three figures. During the ceremonies members of the *nevinbur* . . . "sing" into these bamboos; the sound, carrying underground through the hollow shafts, comes out near Mansip and his wives, who are thus made to seem, to the uninitiated spectators, to be singing.[2]

After the sacrifice of a pig—to ensure the success of the puppet ceremony—four members of the *nevinbur* society danced toward the special shelter of Mansip. Over his head, each man held a small puppet representing one of the sons of Mansip. These were held in such a way that the puppeteers could not be seen and members of the audience were convinced that the figures themselves were dancing. At this point, an elder of the society came out of the fenced enclosure. With a hammer, he smashed the four figures. According to tradition, these had to be destroyed before any new figures could be created.

There followed a long interval of several months during which time society members sequestered themselves inside the ceremonial house and created hundreds of new puppets. When everything was ready, a date and a time were set for the completion of the ceremony. At the designated time, the dancers once again emerged from the men's house into the fenced enclosure; dancing, they held their figures above their heads so that the spectators could see only the puppets. At the conclusion of this dance, a kind of pudding was offered from the exterior of the stockade to two very elaborate puppets. These figures were built so that they could carry the food to their mouths with their hands. Then an old man armed with a spear appeared on the outside of the stockade and strode towards Mansip's shelter. From inside the enclosure a member of the society spoke for Mansip:

MANSIP: Why are you standing there?
OLD MAN: But Grandfather, I'm not doing anything.
MANSIP: My grandson, I can feel your hatred.
OLD MAN: Then why don't you run away?[3]

As he said his final words, the old man took his spear and stabbed Mansip and his two wives. A blood red liquid was made to flow from the puppets while a strange drumming and chanting went on inside the stockade. Society members then set fire to the entire stockade and the

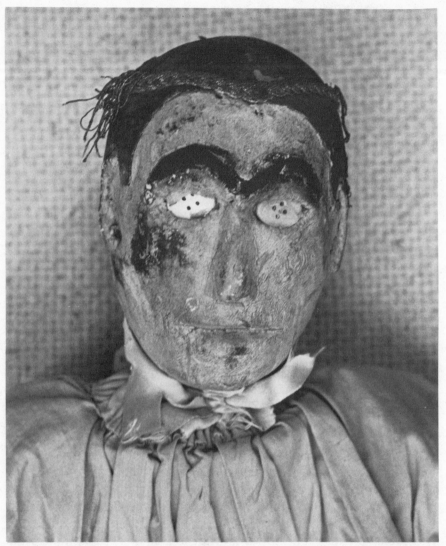

Hula Ki'i **puppet from Hawaii of the late nineteenth or very early twentieth century. Note the shell eyes.** *Courtesy Smithsonian Institution. (Photo by David L. Young)*

three mutilated puppet figures of Mansip and his wives were cast into the flames.

Deacon indicates that similar ceremonies using puppets may have existed in other areas of southern Malekula but due to the extreme secrecy of the rituals, information is difficult to obtain. It should be noted that although Günter Böhmer identifies the figures in the Munich City Puppet Collection as coming from New Caledonia,[4] I have found no evidence of *temes nevinbur* puppets outside of the island of Malekula in the New Hebrides.

In any event, it is clear that the *nevinbur* "puppet show" can in no way be considered simple entertainment.

The extreme sanctity of all parts of this *Nevinbur* ritual is undoubted. It is said that during all the proceedings it is a *newut ilau,* that is a very sacred time, when certain definite *tabus* must be observed. Thus, no one but the initiated may break a stick, cut a coconut, climb a tree, or gather coconuts near the village. Absolute quiet must reign and infringement of any of these *tabus* is punished by death.[5]

A somewhat less sacred form of puppetry is known to have existed on Easter Island. Dating from the time of the powerful island ruler Tuukoihu, the origins and history of the form are shrouded in myth and legend. No one is certain, for example, when or if Tuukoihu actually lived. Apparently, however, in order to help his people tolerate the ever-present problems of famine and starvation, King Tuukoihu manufactured scores of wooden images in the likenesses of well-fed men and women. These marionettes were called *moai miro.* The puppeteer

... arranged them so that they could be hung on a cord all around the roof of his three hundred foot long house; by another cord he kept them whirling around, whilst with a third he could control the movements of their limbs. And when the people crowded round there they saw the little wooden images dancing the *hokohoko* as they gyrated round the roof of Tuukoihu's house. And they laughed as they contrasted this with the picture of famine and the malignance of ghosts that they had seen in the rib-and-thigh-bone memorial images. He had found the true secret of the management of his Easter Islanders. Through all of their history they have loved to live for the moment and forget the hateful things of the past and shut their eyes to the hateful things that might come.[6]

Unfortunately, there is little or no information concerning the history of the *moai miro* after the time of the semilegendary Tuukoihu.

In contrast to the ritual puppets of the New Hebrides and Easter Island, the puppets of Hawaii were used purely for entertainment. They are described by Nathaniel B. Emerson in his book *Unwritten Literature of Hawaii.* It is undoubtedly the best source on the formerly indigenous form of Hawaiian puppetry known as *hula ki'i.*

The origins of the *hula ki'i* are uncertain but performances are known to have continued at least until the time of the fiftieth birthday party of King Kalakaua in the 1880s.

The *hula ki'i* were large hand puppets about one third life size. The heads were more or less realistically carved from soft wood and the costumes were fashioned from a special tapa cloth called *mahuna*. This fabric was perforated with small holes and stained with a copper-colored juice derived from the root bark of the kukui tree.[7]

Emerson characterizes a *hula ki'i* performance in the following way.

> The performer in the hula, who stood behind a screen, by insinuating his hands under the clothing of the marionette, could impart to it such movements as were called for by the action of the play, while at the same time he repeated the words of his part, words supposed to be uttered by the marionette.
>
> The *hula ki'i* was, perhaps, the nearest approximation made by the Hawaiians to a genuine dramatic performance. Its usual instrument of musical accompaniment was the *ipu*. . . . This drumlike object was handled by that division of the performers called the *hoopa'a* who sat in full view of the audience manipulating the *ipu* in a quiet, sentimental manner.[8]

In one *hula ki'i* play, the character Puapuakea challenged the boastful warrior Maka-kú. The first three of a series of contests— javelin throwing, sling shooting, and stone throwing—all resulted in a tie. In the fourth contest—the classical Hawaiian martial art of *lua,* which is similar to but more violent than *jiu-jitsu*—Puapuakea won, after a long struggle, by a scant three points.

During this final contest, they were closely watched by two sisters who fell in love with the heroes and, through a series of amusing episodes, won the affections of the two—at first unwilling—athletes. Finally, the two couples united and settled down to married life.

Evidently, the performances often included a certain amount of interplay between the performers and the spectators.

> One of the marionettes, for instance, points to some one in the audience; whereupon one of the *hoppa'a* asks, "What do you want?" The marionette persists in its pointing. At length the interlocutor, as if divining the marionette's wish, says: "Ah, you want so and so." At this the marionette nods assent and the *hoppa'a* asks again, "Do you wish him to come to you?" The marionette expresses its delight and approval by nods and gestures to the immense satisfaction of the audience, who join in derisive laughter at the expense of the person held up to ridicule.[9]

There were two more characters from the *hula ki'i* who, like the already mentioned Maka-kú and his rival Puapuakea, are similar to stock character types in many of the world's folk plays. There was, for example, the Hawaiian Don Juan, Nihi-aumoe, an ingenious ma-

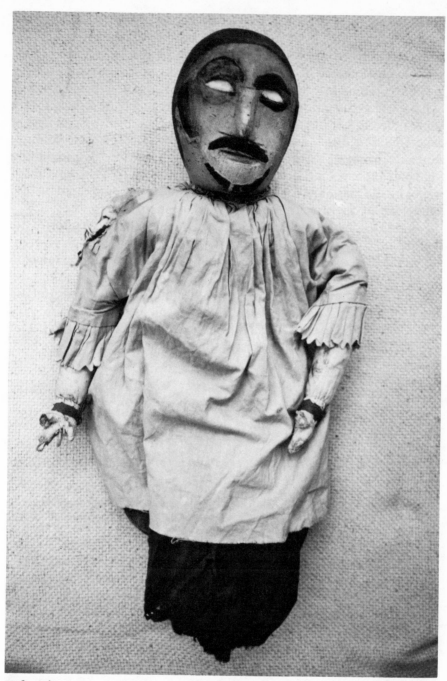

Hula Ki'i puppet from Hawaii with wooden body, eyes of shell, and painted
features. *Courtesy Smithsonian Institution. (Photo by David L. Young)*

nipulator of men and a shrewd seducer of women. His name, appropriately enough, means "to walk softly at midnight." Another important character was the small but vigorous Ki'i-ki'i. The sycophantic marshal of the King, he was always ready to carry out his master's commands, no matter how unappealing they might be.[10]

If we can assume that the songs that accompanied the *hula ki'i* were some reflection of the puppet shows themselves, then we can accept Emerson's analysis and characterize the *hula ki'i* as "gossipy, sarcastic, ironical, scandal mongering, dealing in satire, abuse, hitting right and left at social and personal vices—a cheese of rank flavor that is not to be partaken of too freely. It might be compared to the vaudeville in opera or to the genre picture in art."[11]

Six *hula ki'i* figures are now a permanent part of the collection at the Smithsonian Institution in Washington, D.C. These puppets, originally collected by Emerson, are perhaps the only remaining tangible evidence of the once vigorous tradition of the *hula ki'i*.

Even in today's shrinking and well-explored world, there are still many cultures in the Pacific Islands about which outsiders know very little. Perhaps future research will reveal information about types of puppetry other than the three fascinating, extinct forms that have been discussed in this chapter.

NOTES

1. A. Bernard Deacon, *Malekula: A Vanishing People in the New Hebrides* (London: George Routledge and Sons, 1934), p. 462.
2. Ibid., p. 463.
3. Trans. from Francoise Girard, "Un Theatre de Marionnettes aux Nouvelles-Hebrides:Son Importance Religieuse," *New Hebrides Tribus* (Stuttgart: Linden-Museum, 6, 1956), p. 9.
4. Günter Böhmer. *The Wonderful World of Puppets* (Boston, Plays Inc. 1971), p. 107.
5. Deacon, *Malekula: A Vanishing People in the New Hebrides*, pp. 467–68.
6. J. Macmillan Brown, *The Riddle of the Pacific* (Boston: Small, 1924), p. 141.
7. Nathaniel B. Emerson, *Unwritten Literature of Hawaii* (New York: Charles Tuttle and Co., 1965), p. 92.
8. Ibid.
9. Ibid., p. 93.
10. Ibid., p. 94.
11. Ibid.

10

The Americas
Native and Imported Traditions

No one can be certain of the precise day, year, or century that puppeteers first appeared in the Americas. Nonetheless, it seems reasonable to assume that certain Indian tribes were using articulated toys, moveable masks, and puppets long before European explorers first arrived on the ancient shores of their new world. Early eyewitness accounts come largely from random notes hastily scribbled in the personal diaries of adventurers, settlers, and missionaries. Fuller and more elaborate information was collected in recent years by anthropologists who persuaded aging chiefs and shamans to preserve the scattered memories of their dwindled cultures.

It is known, for example, that the Hopi, a pueblo-dwelling people in what is now northern Arizona, made extensive use of puppetry in some of their rituals. Among the most spectacular of these was their Ceremony of the Great Plumed Snake.

As the members of the Hopi tribe entered the ceremonial area, their eyes gradually became adjusted to the dim and flickering light of a small fire. They could see a number of miniature cornstalks that were set in clay bases and placed about five or six feet in front of a brightly colored cloth that was hung across one end of the ceremonial lodge or *kiva*. Suddenly, a masked dancer appeared in front of the cloth. Musicians hidden behind the backdrop accompanied his dance with drums, songs, and special wind instruments made from dried gourds. Just as the dancer retired behind the cloth, six large snake figures slithered into view, undulating through special holes in the backdrop.

Modern Hopi string operated jumping figures from Arizona and New Mexico. The figure in the center is a kachina clown; the other two are mudheads. *Courtesy Alan G. Cook. (Photo by Alan G. Cook)*

The puppet snakes moved in time to the chanting of the hidden singers and to the eerie howling and moaning of the gourds. Their hawk-feathered crests quivering, they rose off the ground and stretched up and out toward the spectators. They hovered above the cornstalks, twisting and turning in a hypnotic aerial ballet, their sinewy five- or six-foot-long bodies weaving strange patterns in the air. Without warning, the snakes swooped earthward and dashed the cornstalks to the ground. At this signal, the tempo of the music grew more rapid and the howling of the gourds grew louder. The *kiva* vibrated with the prayers and exultations of the worshippers as they shouted, prayed, and threw offerings of cornmeal at the snakes. Slowly, the frenzy subsided, and the ritually appeased snakes retreated until only their heads showed in front of the backcloth. Bulging eyes glowing in the firelight, the snakes were withdrawn as the next part of the ceremony began.

In her book *Rod Puppets and the Human Theatre*, Marjorie Batchelder includes an extensive and fascinating discussion of these Hopi snake puppets.

Their heads are either cut out of cottonwood or made of gourds and are painted, and the protruberant goggle eyes are small buckskin bags tied to the top. Each head bears a medial horn curving forward, sometimes made with joints and at other times solid. A radiating crest of hawk feathers is tied vertically to the back of the head.

The teeth are cut in the gourd or wood of which the head is made and are painted red. The tongue is a leather strap, also painted red, and protrudes from the mouth a considerable distance. The top of the head is black, the bottom white, and these same colors continue along the sides of the body.

The body consists of a central stick, called a backbone, over which extended a covering which is held in place by a series of hoops graduated in size from the neck to the end. The effigy is manipulated by means of the stick, held by a man behind the screen. The "backbone" has a ferule cut in it a few inches back of the neck, and to this ferule are tied a quartz crystal called the heart, and a package which contains seeds of all colors, melon, squash, cotton and other seeds, and a black prayer stick. The body is made of a series of hoops called ribs, over which is stretched cotton cloth painted black above and white below, with a red streak at the dividing line, where there are also other markings and symbols.[1]

In yet another Hopi ritual, string puppets of birds and of maidens realistically grinding corn on small stone slabs figure prominently.

Rituals utilizing puppets seem to have had a dual purpose in Hopi tribal culture. The first was to provide instruction in the great religious stories and legends through the medium of dramatic performance. The second was to provide entertainment. To these ends, both the puppets and the ceremonies in which they were used were carefully—even meticulously—contrived. Whether or not the audience believed that the figures were actually alive is debatable. Bil Baird, for example, has written that it is unlikely that the " . . . Hopi knew how the snakes were activated, or suspected, for that matter, that they were not real spirits. The quality of the illusion and the audience's acceptance of it were such that the strings supporting the dancing snakes could have been an eighth of an inch thick without anyone's noticing."[2] Despite the precautions that were taken to ensure the secrets of performance, it is also possible that at least some spectators had a healthy skepticism with regard to the nature of the puppets. Perhaps, the shows were so impressive that the reality—or unreality—of the figures was simply not an issue among those who were pleased to witness the ceremony again and again over a period of many years.

Much better known than their puppets are the Hopi kachina dolls that are carved from wood to represent ancestral spirits called kachinas. Los Angeles based puppeteer Alan Cook has in his collection three, small, articulated, clay, kachina figures that were

The head of this thirty-one-and-one-half-inch-high Kwakiutl figure is made from two pieces of wood and set on a piece of dowelling. The arms are joined to the body by a strip of leather. The figure moves by means of two spools in the back of the box. During the Tuxwit dance, the box was buried in the floor with only the head of the figure showing. *Courtesy Museum of Anthropology, University of British Columbia.*

This wooden Kwakiutl crab has a spool roller in its underside so that it would scuttle along the floor when pulled. It represents a supernatural ground crab of the woods. *Courtesy Museum of Anthropology, University of British Columbia.*

designed to help acquaint children with the characters and other attributes of various spirits. Because it was feared that the manufacture of such figures was open to misinterpretation by outsiders, the tribe has stopped making them.

Among such Indian tribes as the Haida, Tsimshian, Niska, and Kwakiutl of the Pacific Northwest, puppets were often used in traditional ceremonies. Some of the most interesting research into the puppetry of these peoples was carried out by Robert Bruce Inverarity, who in the early 1930s lived among the Haida of the Queen Charlotte Islands off the coast of British Columbia. It was primarily because the old rituals were no longer practiced that he was able to obtain information about the once extremely secret ceremonies.

At the high point of one Haida ceremony, the figure of a man sprang out of the ground, made a few gestures, and then vanished back into the earth. In another ritual, an otter crawled out of a water-filled hole in the center of the ceremonial house. After playing on the edge of this small pond, he dove back into the water, swam around, and then disappeared beneath its surface.

Great pains were taken to produce such effects.

Strings made of spruce roots ran from the puppet over beams and out on to the roof, or over to blanketed-off corners where the hidden manipulators would wait. The chanted song gave the cue for one manipulator to pull the string, then for another to pull his. In this way, the figure was made to move.[3]

Carved from wood in the shape of a human, this Kwakiutl figure was used in the Tuxwit dance. *Courtesy Museum of Anthropology, University of British Columbia.*

The Museum of Anthropology at the University of British Columbia has in its collection several interesting figures made by the Kwakiutl Indians of the Pacific Northwest. Some of these Kwakiutl puppets are closely related to the previously described Haida figures. Such puppets were placed in specially fashioned boxes. When in use, a trench was dug in the ground, and at the appropriate time during a ceremonial dance, the figures would be made to spring from their boxes up out of the ground, with their arms outspread.[4] The total height of the boxes, with the puppets extended, was thirty-five inches.

Another similar box was of a baby in a cradle; and although it was somewhat larger—three feet five inches long—it was operated in much the same manner. In this case, however, the box or cradle was not buried. When special strings were pulled, the puppet inside the cradle sat up and "appeared to be watching a spinning ball . . . that whirled around on a shaft in the front of the cradle."[5]

The Tsimshian and the Kwakiutl tribes used articulated crabs carved from wood. These crabs were cleverly built so that, as they were pulled sideways, they moved easily on rollers hidden on their undersides. The crackling of their moving parts made them sound like live crabs scuffling along shoreline rocks or leaves.

Perhaps the most dramatic uses of puppetry were closely guarded secrets of Haida shamans, or witch doctors. In one particularly

Made in the shape of an angel, this Kwakiutl figure has a small piece of glass in the center of its forehead and silver foil under its eyes. It was used in the Nunlham dance. *Courtesy Museum of Anthropology, University of British Columbia.*

167

These hand puppets were made in the early 1960s in Alert Bay, British Columbia, by Ellen Neel. *Courtesy Alan G. Cook. (Photo by Alan G. Cook)*

dramatic—and gruesome—ceremony, they placed a man on the ground and apparently cut off his head. Then, as the spectators watched, the bloodied head mysteriously crept along the ground away from its body. After one of the shamans announced that the man would be healed, the head slithered back toward the body. As soon as it touched his neck, the man leapt up, obviously none the worse for the experience. What actually happened was:

The witch doctors gathered around the man on the ground so that the actual cutting could not be seen, but the audience heard about it in

Punch, Judy, and Baby, possibly American. *Courtesy Alan G. Cook. (Photo by Alan G. Cook)*

the song. The victim, hidden under a blanket, and in secret with the operators, lowered his head into a pit so that when the group about him drew apart, he appeared to be decapitated. A carved replica of his head was revealed on the ground. Its neck had been smeared with fresh animal blood kept ready in a bag of seal bladder. A manipulator in a ditch in the ground made the head move. When the witch doctor proclaimed that the victim would be brought back to life, the head was brought towards his neck, the group crowded around as if in attention and hid the final movement. The wooden head was pulled out of sight; the victim got up, restored and whole![6]

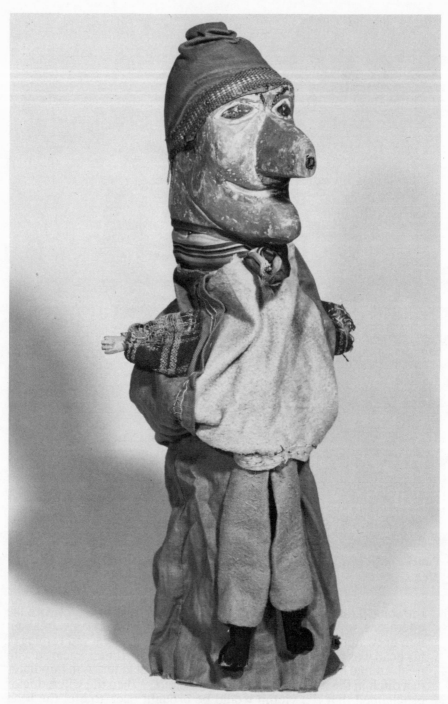

Late eighteenth-century American Punch. *Courtesy Margo Lovelace. (Photo by David L. Young)*

Other Indian tribes in many areas of both North and South America used puppets. In 1655, an Iroquois medicine man demonstrated the strength of his magic herbs by removing an apparently dead squirrel from his pouch and rubbing it with the herbs. Then, he manipulated

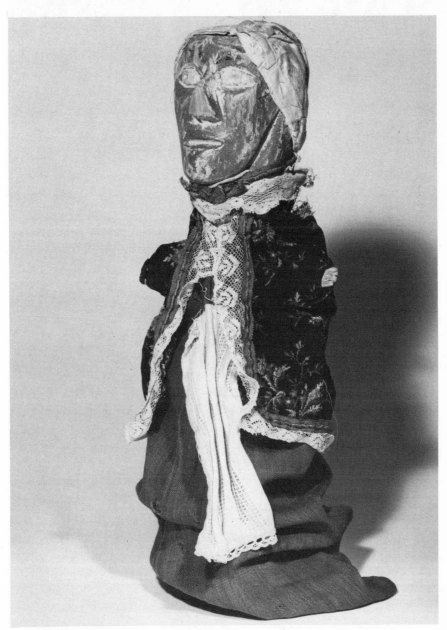

Late eighteenth-century American Judy. *Courtesy Margo Lovelace. (Photo by David L. Young)*

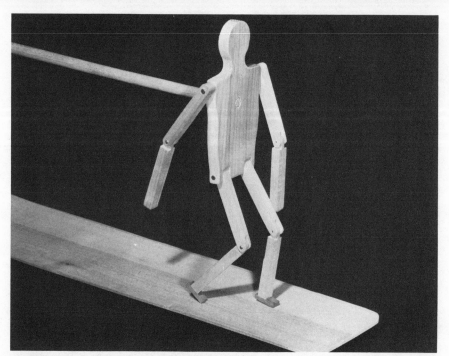

Simple dancing puppet used as a rhythm instrument. From Pennsylvania.
Author's collection. (Photo by David L. Young)

A group of dissecting skeletons and other figures. *Courtesy Alan G. Cook.*
(Photo by Alan G. Cook)

Mantell Mannequins and a Mantell proscenium. The company, which was popular from about 1903 to 1940, was under the direction of Len Ayres. The trunk at left is one of several that were used to ship the Mantell show all around the world. *Courtesy Alan G. Cook. (Photo by Alan G. Cook)*

strings concealed in the puppet squirrel's tail and made it jump in and out of the pouch as though it were alive.[7] Paul McPharlin, in *The Puppet Theatre in America,* documented the use of a small puppet by a Toltec medicine man in Mexico sometime before 1590.[8] He also recounts how a Spanish magician *cum* puppeteer accompanied Hernando Cortes when he left Tenochititlan—now Mexico City—in 1524 to search for gold in the Honduras.[9] McPharlin believes that such early European puppeteers may have influenced Indian puppets but there is simply not enough information for firm judgment.

From the scattered accounts available, it would be difficult to piece together a genuine history of early colonial and Indian puppetry. Existing records, although often fascinating, are simply not very complete.

There is, however, a good deal of information about the types and forms of puppetry that were brought by immigrants to the New World.

During the eighteenth and nineteenth centuries, many European and Oriental puppeteers moved to the Americas, bringing with them their own skills, styles, and traditions of puppetry: the Paladins of Sicily, Karagoz from Greece and Turkey, Punch and Judy from England, and shadow figures from China. Some of the performers toured with circuses, many took to the road on their own, and still others settled in

Mantell Mannequin juggler. *Courtesy Alan G. Cook. (Photo by Alan G. Cook)*

major cities where the old forms were preserved in the original languages and styles—sometimes on a professional and more usually on a semiprofessional or amateur basis. The lives and fortunes of some of these men and women have been carefully chronicled in McPharlin's *The Puppet Theatre in America*.

In North and South America, as in Europe, an increasing number of vaudeville-style troupes became popular after 1860. Bil Baird has

Mantell Mannequin jockies at the racetrack. *Courtesy Alan G. Cook. (Photo by Alan G. Cook)*

noted that, with their reliance on stock characters and standard bits of stage business, these traveling puppet shows were deeply rooted in the folk art tradition.[10] Large English companies such as Bullock's, Till's, Clunn-Lewis's, Barnard's, and Holden's gained widespread popularity and were enormously influential particularly in the United States and Canada.

These companies used puppets in a combination circus and vaudeville-style format. Trick figures were particularly popular in these traveling performances and included various kinds of puppet clowns, acrobats, trapeze artists, jugglers, and animals.

Some exceptionally spectacular trick figures became standard characters. In addition to the Grand Turk and the Mère Gigogne figures, which were described in the chapter on European puppets, a figure known as the dissecting skeleton was particularly popular. It would appear on stage and begin to dance. As the audience watched, first the head and then an arm would fly up and out of sight while the remaining bones continued to dance. Piece by piece the whole puppet would disappear and as the audience applauded, the bones would fly back together just in time for the puppet to take its final bow. Other

175

Roger Westley's opera singer and pianist were well known in West Coast nightclubs during the 1940s. Similar type figures have been popular since the late ninteenth century. *Courtesy Alan G. Cook. (Photo by Alan G. Cook)*

commonly featured performers were a lady who turned into a balloon and an elegant ostrich that trotted onto the stage, sat down, and laid an egg out of which hatched an enormous snake that frightened the ostrich off the stage. Additional favorites were a long-haired piano player and a large-mouthed, heavily bosomed opera singer. Naturally, no show was complete without its chorus line—usually, four or five dancing puppets that could be operated by a single control. Two popular American companies, Walter Deaves and the Mantells, also used puppet audiences whose comic antics and reactions were an important part of their performances.

These fast-paced puppet variety shows never left a figure onstage long enough to outlive its welcome. As a result, a company needed a large number of puppet characters. Bil Baird recalls seeing the Mantell's show when he was still a boy: " 'Mantell's Marionette Hippodrome', one early poster read. 'Fairyland Transformation—Big Scenic Novelty—Seventeen Gorgeous Drop Curtains—Forty-Five Elegant Talking-Acting Figures in a Comical Pantomime.' "[11]

After 1850, traveling circus and vaudeville-style puppet shows were almost as popular in Central and South America as they were in

This Jewell Mannequin Indian has a leather headdress cut to look like feathers. *Courtesy Josie Robbins. (Photo by Alan G. Cook)*

These toy puppets were all made in Mexico during the 1960s. The chief materials are clay, cornhusks, and papier-mâché. *Courtesy Alan G. Cook (Photo by Alan G. Cook)*

This hand puppet of a black man may have been used as a servant in an American Punch and Judy show. *Courtesy Alan G. Cook. (Photo by Alan G. Cook)*

Canada and the United States. The Latin American performances usually included bull fighters and Spanish dancers but were otherwise quite similar to their North American and European counterparts. Such shows existed along with localized puppet traditions in the style of Punch and Judy and imported traditions such as the Sicilian marionettes.

Mexico was home to many puppet theaters, from sophisticated professional companies to village craftsmen who turned out carefully made but nonetheless inexpensive toy figures. Descriptions of many of these objects can be found in Roberto Lago's *Mexican Folk Puppets:*

This antique ventriloqual figure by Shaw has wooden hands and a papier-mâché body. The mouth and the eyes are movable. *Courtesy Alan G. Cook. (Photo by Alan G. Cook)*

Traditional and Modern, which is now quite difficult to find. Fortunately, Paul McPharlin included an interesting quotation from it in *The Puppet Theatre in America*.

179

What beautifully carved and colored wooden horses came from Irapuato! . . . Strings pass down their supporting sticks to move their heads, legs and the arms of the riders. From Salamanca, come monkeys on a pole and Apache guitarists, liveliest of toys. The capital provides jumping-jack skeletons or caricatures of political personages (appropriately pulled by strings) all cut from cardboard. Then there are the delicate figures of Puebla, whose form is legion, and the sun-baked clay puppets of Toluca and Metepec, crude but teeming with earthy vigor. Whether made from clay, wood, rags or cornhusks, these creatures of fantasy, birds and animals, half-human monkeys, witches, demons and ghosts, have the quality of seeming alive.[12]

During the late nineteenth and early twentieth centuries, another form of puppetry, ventriloquism, became particularly popular in the music halls and vaudeville theaters of Europe and the Americas. Ventriloqual figures are relatively complicated puppets that often have movable mouths, eyes, eyelids, eyebrows, and ears.

The art of the ventriloquist involves the production of a suitable voice and personality for the figure. The famous technique of "throwing the voice" means that the performer must learn to speak with minimal lip movement. More importantly, the ventriloquist learns to control the attention of the spectators so that they are always looking in the right place at the right time.

In Europe and the United States, ventriloquism has been a traditional form of entertainment for the last one hundred years—although as a technique it is far older. In the United States, the form has become particularly popular in nightclubs and on television. It is due largely to the fame of the American ventriloquist Edgar Bergen and his puppet friend, Charlie McCarthy, that ventriloquism became extremely popular during the late 1930s and early 1940s. So strongly were their stage personalities established that, for many years, Bergen and McCarthy were the stars of a highly successful *radio* show—an extraordinary achievement for an essentially visual act!

Because of the large number of American ventriloquists, it is not surprising that the most complete collection of ventriloqual figures in the world is housed in the United States. Collected by the late businessman W. S. Bergen—no relation to Edgar—the figures are now on display at the Vent Haven Museum, Inc., Fort Mitchell, Kentucky, in the building that was formerly the home of Mr. Bergen. Fortunately, ventriloquism is still as popular as it ever was and there seems no danger of it disappearing.

During the early 1930s, the United States government sponsored a large number of puppet theater companies. As a result, many people

W.P.A. oyster puppet from Pennsylvania, used in a production of *Alice in* *Wonderland. Courtesy Margo Lovelace. (Photo by David L. Young)*

thought that the way was being laid for a national puppet theater or at least a new grassroots surge of activity in puppet theater. But despite the fact that a vast number of shows were produced, the projects did not provide the nation with any new folk puppet style. Nonetheless, with hundreds of people producing shows on similar subjects with similar style puppets, the W.P.A. came remarkably close to fostering a national tradition of folk puppetry in the United States.

On March 13, 1933, the Congress of the United States passed the first Relief Act in order to help create jobs for the unemployed. During the following two years, a number of similar programs were created. These included the Federal Emergency Relief Administration and the Civil Works Administration. All of these projects were in some measure superceded by the Works Progress Administration, which was legislated into existence on April 8, 1935. From 1933 to 1941, these programs sponsored a large number of puppet theater projects. Some of them were carried out under the supervision of professional puppeteers with considerable reputations such as Paul McPharlin, Remo Bufano, Tony Sarg, Robert Bromley, and Ralph Chessé. Many puppet shows were produced by the Federal Theatre, an administrative unit of the W.P.A. At one point, in addition to its many other activities, the Federal Theatre provided funds and organizational support for twenty producing puppet theaters that collectively employed three hundred and fifty performers and technicians. More than one hundred shows a week were presented to audiences averaging four hundred people. Most of the productions used hand or string puppets. The plays were usually adaptations of well-known stories such as "Cinderella," "Ali Baba and the Forty Thieves," "Hansel and Gretel," or "Sleeping Beauty." Original plays were presented somewhat less frequently. A list of these productions can be found in the appendix of Hallie Flanigan's book *Arena: The History of the Federal Theatre*. In addition, a great deal of material can be found in the Federal Theater Collection housed at George Mason University in Fairfax, Virginia.

As an adjunct to the performing troupes, puppeteers developed various kinds of educational extension programs. Only some of these activities were financed by the Federal Theatre. Work in educational puppetry was sponsored primarily by the W.P.A. Recreation Project and other groups under W.P.A. jurisdiction. These projects involved helping hospitals, churches, museums, settlement houses, playground supervisors, and teachers' organizations make and perform with puppets on an amateur level. Often, such amateur groups were under the loose supervision of seasoned, professional puppeteers, and literally thousands of figures were made—from simple hand puppets to shadow puppets to large and complicated marionettes.

In *The Puppet Theatre in America*, Paul McPharlin wrote:

During the years of the W.P.A., 1934–1941, thousands of puppet shows were given free to the public by workers trained as puppeteers while on relief rolls. At one time, there were more W.P.A. puppeteers in New York City alone than there had

W.P.A. Hansel and the Woodcutter from Pittsburgh, Pennsylvania, used in production of *Hansel and Gretel. Author's collection. (Photo by David L. Young)*

previously been in the entire United States. Some of the shows were done by the Theatre Project, others by the Recreation Project; a few puppets were even made by art projects to turn over to workers on community chest campaigns. Unfortunately, the existence of all these projects was so brief or so vexed by problems extraneous to puppetry that little survived from them. I wonder what became of all the hundreds of puppets that were made.[13]

In point of fact, many W.P.A. puppets were lost or destroyed, but

Group of W.P.A. hand puppets from Pennsylvania used in a production of *Aladdin and His Lamp. Courtesy Margo Lovelace. (Photos by David L. Young)*

because puppets have a sometimes charming and often mystical claim on the pretense of life, many have survived. Some have found their way into major public and private collections. Others were packed up and stored away—for grandchildren, perhaps. Or, because few people could predict their eventual monetary value, they were simply put away and forgotten.

Often, the dusty boxes of puppets were rediscovered by people who finally found time to straighten up the old attic, garage, or basement. Since many of the figures were created for educational purposes, large numbers of puppets were made in the form of toothbrushes, or fruits and vegetables, while others depicted characters from popular children's stories. Costs were such an important consideration that there were few lavishly made puppets or figures made from unusual or expensive materials such as rubber or plastics. W.P.A. puppets were usually made from cloth, papier-mâché, paint, and wood.

Because of the wide variety in the interests and abilities of those who created puppets and puppet shows under the auspices of the W.P.A., there is no standard quality to W.P.A. figures. Some are exquisitely fashioned, others are crudely put together. Nonetheless, all of them are fascinating reminders of an intriguing period in the social and cultural history of the United States of America.

The history of traditional and folk puppetry in the Americas is peculiar. The native American forms were destroyed, in many cases, even before they were discovered by the white settlers. And the folk puppetry of the new Americans was strongly based on the traditional theaters of their Asian, Middle Eastern, or European ancestors. It is this fact that led Bil Baird to observe that "there has been no long, single tradition of American puppetry."[14]

Nonetheless, it is certain that puppet theater will continue to play a vital role in the entertainment and education of adults and children throughout the Americas. The present surge of interest in puppetry, created and fed largely through the medium of television, may well be the source of future traditions—traditions that can exist only when they are nurtured by an abiding love and respect for the timeless art of puppet theater.

NOTES

1. Marjorie Batchelder, *Rod Puppets and the Human Theatre* (Columbus: Ohio Univ. Press, 1947), p. 182.
2. Bil Baird, *The Art of the Puppet* (New York: Macmillan, 1965), p. 31.
3. Robert Bruce Inverarity, *A Manual of Puppetry* (Portland: Binfords and Mort, 1936), p. 204.
4. Audrey Hawthorne, *Art of the Kwakiutl Indians* (Seattle: Univ. of Washington Press, 1967), p. 73.
5. Ibid.
6. Inverarity, *A Manual of Puppetry*, p. 205.
7. Paul McPharlin, *The Puppet Theatre in America* (Boston: Plays, Inc., 1949), p. 9.
8. Ibid.
9. Ibid., p. 6.
10. Baird, *The Art of the Puppet*, p. 161.
11. Ibid., p. 160.
12. Roberto Lago, quoted in *The Puppet Theatre in America*, p. 254.
13. McPharlin, *The Puppet Theatre in America*, pp. 370–71.
14. Baird, *The Art of the Puppet*, p. 220.

Conclusion

It is impossible to come to any firm conclusion about the nature and future of traditional and folk puppetry around the world. Undoubtedly, there would have been some intellectual satisfaction in summing it all up; in being able to say that folk puppetry is everywhere alive and well or that most traditional puppet theaters are either dead or dying. But the situation is more complicated than that. It is unlikely, for example, that the *hula ki'i* of Hawaii or the *moai miro* of Easter Island will ever be revived. On the other hand, Punch and Judy are more popular than ever and the traditional puppet styles in such places as China and Indonesia do not seem to be in any immediate danger.

For the past one hundred and fifty years or so, people and their cultures have been changing with increasing rapidity. Traditional and folk puppeteers have had to redouble their efforts to keep pace with the world around them. Through exposure to television and cinema, modern audiences have grown accustomed to seeing the work of some of the world's finest puppet theater artists. As a result, even relatively unsophisticated spectators quickly become impatient with the poor acting or imprecise manipulation of less than expert performers.

By the same token, styles of puppetry that can no longer appeal to very many people fade from existence. The public tires of puppeteers who rigorously adhere to the performance traditions of their ancestors yet fail to adapt to the developing tastes of their audiences.

Despite these complications, puppetry is growing more and more popular throughout the world. The traditional and folk puppet styles discussed in this book, as well as the creative achievements of a few extraordinary individuals, have all contributed to the development of the art of puppet theater: an art that is destined to thrive for as long as humankind endures.

Selected Bibliography

Änd, Metin. *A History of Theatre and Popular Entertainment in Turkey*. Ankara: Forum, 1963.

Anderson, Madge. *Heroes of the Puppet Stage*. New York: Harcourt, Brace and World, 1923.

Anon. "Chinese Puppet History." Unpublished material. Kuangchu Program Service: Taipei, 1974.

Arnott, Peter. *Plays Without People*. Bloomington: Indiana University Press, 1964.

Baird, Bil. *The Art of the Puppet*. New York: Macmillan, 1965.

Batchelder, Marjorie. *Rod Puppets and the Human Theatre*. Columbus: Ohio University Press, 1947.

Belo, Jane. *Traditional Balinese Culture*. New York: Columbia University Press, 1970.

Benegal, Som, ed. *Puppet Theatre Around the World*. Bharatya Natya Sangh: New Delhi, 1960.

Binghan, Jane. "History of Marionettes," *Leisure* (4) May 1937.

Blackham, Olive. *Shadow Puppets*. London: Rockliff, 1960.

Boehn, Max Von. *Puppets and Automata*. Trans. Josephine Nicoll. New York: Dover, 1972.

Böhmer, Günter. *The Wonderful World of Puppets*. Trans. Gerald Morice. Boston: Plays, Inc., 1971.

Brandon, James. *On Thrones of Gold*. Cambridge, Mass.: Harvard Univ. Press, 1970.

Brown, J. Macmillan. *The Riddle of the Pacific*. Boston: Small, 1924.

Caimi, Giulio. *Karagiozi ou la Comédie Greque dans l'Âme du Théâtre d'Ombres*. Athens: Hellinkies Teches, 1935.

Chambers, E. K. *The Medieval Stage, Vol. II*. London: Oxford, 1903.

Chesnais, Jacques. "Marionnettes Africaines," *World Theatre* 14:5 (1965).

Contractor, Meher (Mrs.), ed. *Marg: A Magazine of the Arts* 21:3 (1968). Bombay: Marg Publications.

Cornevin, R. *Le Théâtre en Afrique Noire et à Madagascar.* Paris: Le Livre Africaine, 1970.

Covarrubais, Miguel. *Island of Bali.* New York: Knopf, 1947.

Cowan, H. W. *Asia.* Boston: Little, Brown and Co., 1929.

Craig, Edward Gordon. "History of Marionette Stage, *Marionette* 1:55–57 (March 1918).

———. "A Brief History of Puppetry," *Marionette* 1:152–54 (June 1918).

———. "Brief History of Puppetry," *Marionette* 1:171–74 (December 1918).

Cueto, L. V., and Lago, R. "Origin and History of Puppetry in Mexico," *Scholastic Arts* 47(May 1948).

Crothers, J. Frances. *The Puppeteer's Library Guide. Vol. I.* Metuchen, N.J.: Scarecrow Press, 1971.

Deacon, A. Bernard. *Malekula: A Vanishing People in the New Hebrides.* London: Geo. Routledge and Sons, 1934.

Emerson, Nathaniel. *Unwritten Literature of Hawaii.* New York: Charles Tuttle, 1965.

Flanigan. Hallie. *Arena: The History of the Federal Theatre.* New York: Benjamin Blom, 1965.

Galvez, José. "Puppets of Yore in Peru," *Turismo* (January 1938).

Gaskill, G. E., and Nolde, J. (compilers). *Far Eastern Bibliography.* Ithaca: Cornell Univ. Press, 1951.

"Giant Puppets for *Barong Landog*," *Theatre Arts* 20:604 (August 1936).

Girard, Françoise. "Un Théâtre de Marionnettes aux Nouvelles Hébrides: Son Importance Religieuse," *New Hebrides Tribus.* Stuttgart: Linden-Museum, Vol. 6. 1956.

Goldwater, Robert. *Bambara Sculpture from the Western Sudan.* New York: University Publishers, 1960.

———. *Traditional Art of the African Nations in the Museum of Primitive Art.* New York: University Publishers, 1961.

Gregorovius, Ferdinand. "Roman Marionettes," *Marionette* 1:184–94 (December 1918).

Guiart, Jean. "Les Effigies Religieuse des Nouvelles-Hébrides," *Societé des Oceanistes Journal* 5 (1949).

———. *The Arts of the South Pacific.* Trans. Anthony Christie. New York: Golden Press, 1963.

Hadr'solseno, Harsano. *Wayang and Education.* Djakarta: Ministry of Education and Culture, 1955.

Hartnoll, Phyllis. "Malaya," *Oxford Companion to the Theatre.* Oxford: Oxford Univ. Press, 1967.

Havemayer, Loomis. *The Drama of Savage Peoples.* New Haven: Yale Univ. Press, 1916.

Hawthorn, Audrey. *Art of the Kwakiutl Indians*. Seattle: Univ. of Washington Press, 1967.

Herald, E. *The Art of Africa; Tribal Masks*. London: Paul Hamlyn, 1967.

Hironaga, Shuzaburo. *Bunraku: Japan's Unique Puppet Theatre*. Tokyo: Tokyo News Service, 1964.

Holt, Claire. *Art in Indonesia: Continuities and Change*. Ithaca: Cornell Univ. Press, 1967.

Hover, Otto. *Javanese Shadow Stage*. New York: In Orient, 1923.

Inverarity, Robert Bruce. *A Manual of Puppetry*. Portland: Binfords and Mort, 1936.

———. *Art of the Northwest Coast Indians*. Berkeley, Univ. of Calif. Press, 1950.

Joseph, Mrs. Helen Haiman. *Book of Marionettes*. New York: Viking, 1929.

Keene, Donald. *Bunraku: The Art of the Japanese Puppet Theatre*. Palo Alto: Kodansha International Press, 1965.

Kennard, Joseph Spencer. *Masks and Marionettes*. New York: Macmillan, 1935.

Kerdchouay, Euayporn and Smithies, Michael. "Giant Shadow Play of Thailand," *Orientations* (August 1973).

Kirby, Michael, ed. "The 'Puppet' Issue," *The Drama Review* 16(1972).

Kudret, Cevdet. "Karagoz in the Culture of Turkey," Part I., Trans. Caroljean Kier. *The Puppetry Journal* 24: 1(1972).

———. "Karagoz in the Culture of Turkey," Part II., Trans. Caroljean Kier. *The Puppetry Journal* 24: 2(1972).

Lago, Roberto. *Mexican Folk Puppets: Traditional and Modern*. Detroit: Puppetry Imprints, 1941.

Landau, Jacob. "Arab Shadow Play," *Atlantic Monthly* (October 1956).

———. *Shadow Plays in the Near East*. Jeruselem: Palestine Institute of Folklore and Ethnology, 1947.

———. *Studies in the Arab Theatre and Cinema*. Philadelphia: Univ. of Pennsylvania Press, 1958.

Laufer, Berthold. *Oriental Theatricals*. Chicago: Field Museum of Natural History, 1923.

Lobl, Muriel Broadman. "Punch," *Saturday Review* (December 1972).

Luizinger, Elsy. *Africa: The Art of the Negro Peoples*. New York: McGraw Hill, 1960.

Lupi, Father Mariantonio. "Dissertation on the Marionettes of the Ancients" *Marionette* 1:55–62 (June 1918).

Magnin, Charles. *Histoire des Marionnettes en Europe*. Paris: 1862.

Maindron, Ernest. *Marionnettes et Guignols à travers les Âges*. Paris: 1900.

Malik, Jan. *Puppetry in Czechoslovakia*. New York: Universal Distributors, 1948.

189

Malkin, Michael R. "A Critical Perspective on Puppetry as Theatre Art," *The Puppetry Journal* (August-September 1975).

———. "Chinese Hand Puppets," *The Antiques Journal* 30:3 (March 1975).

———. "Collecting Indian Puppets," *The Antiques Journal* 29:8 (August 1974).

———. "Collecting Indonesian Puppets," *The Antiques Journal* 30:11 (November 1975).

———. "Turkish Shadow Puppets," *The Antiques Journal* 29:12 (December 1974).

———. "W.P.A. Puppets," *The Antiques Journal* 31:3 (March 1976).

March, Benjamin. *Chinese Shadow Figure Plays and Their Making*. Detroit: Puppetry Imprints, 1938.

Martinovitch, Nicholas M. *The Turkish Theatre*. New York: Benjamin Blom, 1968.

McPharlin, Paul. *The Puppet Theatre in America*. Boston: Plays, Inc., 1949.

Meyers, John Bernard. "Puppets Probably Preceded People on World's Stages." *Smithsonian* 6:2 (May 1975).

Nieulescu, Margaret, ed. *Puppet Theatres of the Modern World*. Trans. Ewald Osers and Elizabeth Strick. Boston: Plays, Inc., 1961.

Obraztsov, Sergei. *The Chinese Puppet Theatre*. Trans. J. T. MacDermott. London: Faber and Faber, 1961.

Philpott, A. R. *Dictionary of Puppetry*. Boston: Plays, Inc., 1969.

Ransome, Grace Greenleaf. *Puppets and Shadows: A Bibliography*. Boston: Faxon, 1931.

Ridgeway, William. *The Dramas and Dramatic Dances of Non-European Races*. Cambridge: Cambridge Univ. Press, 1915.

Sang-Su, Choe. *Korea: A Study of the Korean Puppet Play*. Seoul: Korean Folklore Studies Series; Korea Books Publishing Co., 1961.

Scott, A. C. *The Puppet Theatre of Japan*. Portland, Vt.: Charles E. Tuttle, 1963.

Sibbuld, Reginald. *Marionettes in the North of France*. Philadelphia: Univ. of Pennsylvania Press, 1936.

Sieber, Roy and Rubin, Arnold. *Sculpture of Black Africa: The Paul Dishman Collection*. Los Angeles: L.A. County Museum of Art, 1968.

Simmen, René. *The World of Puppets*. New York: Thomas Y. Crowell Company, 1975.

Sitwell, S. *Dramas and Dance Cycles of the Islands*. London: Faber and Faber, 1947.

Siyasvusgil, Sabri Esat. *Karagöz*. Ankara: Turkish Press, Broadcasting and Tourist Dept., 1955.

Speaight, George. *History of the English Puppet Theatre*. London: Harrap, 1955.

———. *History of the English Toy Theatre*. Boston: Plays, Inc., 1965.

———. *Punch and Judy: A History*. Boston: Plays, Inc., 1970.

Talbot, P. Amaury. *Life in Southern Nigeria*. New York: Barnes and Noble, 1967.

Tilakasiri, J. *The Puppet Theatre of Asia*. Ceylon: Dept. of Cultural Affairs, 1969.

Tuyh, Leh Vinh. "Vietnam's Terrestrial and Aquatic Puppets," *World Theatre* 14:5 (1965).

Wimsatt, Genevieve Blanche. *Chinese Shadow Shows*. Cambridge, Mass.: Harvard Univ. Press, 1936.

Index